CAMPER COOKERY

Richard Bock

CAMPER COOKERY

Illustrations by Jan Upp

LORENZ
PRESS

501 EAST THIRD STREET • DAYTON • OHIO • 45401

ISBN: 0-89328-008-9

Lorenz Press, Inc.
501 E. Third St.
Dayton, Ohio 45401

Contents

Appetizers and Dips

Soups

Salads

Salads (Cont.)

Sandwiches

Pasta and Rice

Eggs and Cheese

Seafood

Seafood (Cont.)

Meats

Poultry

Poultry (Cont.)

Vegetables

Sauces

Desserts

Introduction

This cookbook is for all those who don't want to leave behind the pleasures of good eating when they head for the wide open spaces. Whether you're taking your motor home, camper, or trailer on a months-long transcontinental trip, or just on a weekend visit to your favorite fishing spot, the quality of your meals is going to have a lot to do with the quality of the trip itself. Relaxation, fresh air, and exercise cause appetites to flourish, which means that good food—and plenty of it—is going to be in constant demand. At the same time, traveling in a motor home means one thing above all else: freedom! And no cook wants to escape the daily routine only to spend a vacation tied to the kitchen. Quick, simple meals are fine for a day or two, but a steady diet of hamburgers will please no one.

The recipes in this cookbook have been chosen to enable you to get out of the kitchen in record time while still providing varied, exciting, and delicious meals that the whole family will enjoy. They represent classic international fare, popular regional dishes from all areas of the United States, and traditional meals that have been given a new twist. There are recipes for main meals and for little treats to serve during that happy hour at the end of the day when campers like to get together for convivial visits. All the recipes have been written with the challenges of the mobile home kitchen in mind—limited storage space, limited equipment, and a scaled-down inventory of accessible ingredients.

In short, these recipes will enable you to cook like a gourmet while living the relaxed, carefree life all mobilehomers are looking for.

Equipment

Your bags are packed, your maps are marked, you're ready to go zooming off into the wild blue (or green) yonder. Or are you? Before you drive away, take a look at the checklist below to make sure you're not forgetting something you might miss in a crucial moment. Space and weight are the two most important limitations on what you'll be able to carry. Cooking equipment wherever possible should do double duty—take frying pans that can be used for boiling, bowls that can be used for serving as well as for mixing and storage, saucepans that can double for frying pans. When selecting your mobile home kitchen equipment, always look for "nestability." Camping goods stores stock a wide variety of nesting pots that fit one inside the other, saving storage space while giving you a number of different sized pots. Nesting bowls are also available, as are cups which can easily be stacked. *All* pots, frying pans and bowls should have tightly fitted lids, both to cut down on heat loss and to prevent steam and cooking vapors from filling your camper.

The recipes in this book have been selected for their adaptability to all types of equipment, and with an eye toward using as little equipment as possible. If you carry with you the items listed below, you'll have no trouble carrying off the preparation of all the meals in this book with a minimum of fuss and bother. But think about each item on the list carefully, and decide if your particular needs require it. If not, omit it—you'll have one less item to carry and a little extra room for your own favorite road gear—or maybe just a little extra room. And once you make up your list, put it away in a safe place in your camper so you can just pull it out when you get ready for your next trip.

Set of nested cooking utensils (saucepans, frying pans, coffee pot, plates and cups—available at Boy Scout and camping centers)

Set of nested plastic bowls with tight fitting covers (for mixing, storing, and serving)

Fruit juice container

Griddle

Muffin tin(s)

Range broiler pan and grid

8" x 8" x 2" aluminum baking pan

9" x 9" x 2" aluminum baking pan

13½" x 9" x 2" aluminum baking pan

14" x 10" aluminum cookie sheet

9" x 5" x 3" loaf pan

8" x 9" aluminum pie pan

2-quart casserole

Can and bottle openers

Cooking fork

Grater

Hot pan holders

Kitchen shears

Knives: 1 French chef's knife, 1 medium slicer, 1 paring knife

Meat thermometer

Minute timer

Nested measuring cups

Nested measuring spoons

Pancake turner

Potato nails (to shorten potato baking time)

Rubber scraper

Small cutting board

Strainer

Tongs

Vegetable brush

Vegetable peeler

Wire whisk

Wooden spoons

Cups or mugs

Glasses

Plates

Stainless steel flatware

Aluminum foil

Cleanser

Cleansing tissues

Dish towels

Dishpan and drainer

Dishwashing detergent

Hand soap

Paper napkins

Paper towels

Plastic bags (for food storage, shell collecting, wet swimsuits, etc.)

Scouring pads

Sponges (better than dishcloths, as they are less likely to sour)

Toilet tissue

Wooden matches

In addition to this basic kitchenware, many families take a small barbecue grill for those evenings when they feel like cooking outdoors. Several collapsible models that will save you space are now on the market; you should consider these when fitting out your camper. Japanese hibachis also are popular. A small insulated cooler or ice chest is handy, no matter how much space you may have in your refrigerator. Water and fruit juices may be frozen at home and placed in the cooler with packages of frozen foods to cool canned soft drinks, meats, and perishables. As the water or juice melts, it can be used for drinking.

Kitchen Hints

Experience is the only teacher when it comes to learning to use your mobile home kitchen most efficiently. Some general tips, however, may help you keep the limited space of your kitchen ship-shape—a must when traveling.

• Wash and dry salad greens at home before your trip. Tear them into bite-sized pieces and store them in small plastic bags. The bags make good fillers for the refrigerator or cooler, and the greens will be ready for use when needed.

• For the last four or five days before you leave for a long trip, prepare at least one meal a day. Freeze the dishes and use each one as it thaws. This not only will leave you more space for staples and perishables, but also will cut down on the time you'll have to spend in the kitchen.

• Prepare a supply of hamburger patties at home. Stack them in a plastic juice container, using waxed paper to separate the patties. Keep them refrigerated until you need them.

• Packages of dried fruit take little storage space. They can be simmered with water and sugar for a delightful snack and used in many recipes.

• Empty "stackable" potato chip cans can be cleaned and used for handy storage of flour, sugar, and grains. Being thin and tall, they take less space than the typical short flour containers.

• Remember that the boiling point of water drops 2 degrees for each 1,000 feet of altitude. If you'll be camping in the mountains, food will have to be cooked longer and additional water may be needed (when cooking rice, for instance).

• Freeze chicken legs and thighs in plastic bags to be used when needed.

• Plan your meals several days ahead and stock canned goods and staples in order of use. Always store the heaviest items as close to the floor of your camper as possible. Proper weight distribution is important in all storage areas of the camper.

• Keep an inventory of canned and dry foods that can be easily checked when restocking.

• Keep an adequate supply of dehydrated onions, parsley, and green peppers on hand as substitutes for their fresh counterparts in many recipes.

• A well-stocked spice rack is indispensable for extended trips. There are many pre-selected spice and condiment collections on the market that will help you add that little something extra to each meal.

• Don't throw away coffee cans with plastic lids. They make excellent storage bins for everything from utensils to dry goods.

Safety Tips

• Make sure there are no loose window curtains, paper towels, or other inflammable substances near the cooking area. Keep a small portable fire extinguisher handy in the kitchen.

• Never cook while driving unless the cooking utensil is firmly anchored with clamps specially made for this purpose. Such clamps are available from any mobile home supply store.

Charcoaling—By the Rules

Lighting the fire

Line the grill with heavy-duty aluminum foil—for faster cooking and easier cleanup later on.

Stack the briquets in a pyramid. They'll light faster with air circulating around them.

Use a good starter. Try the electric or chimney type, or choose a liquid, jelly, or solid fibrous cubes.

Be patient. Let the briquets burn to just the right stage before you start to cook. Generally they'll require 20 to 40 minutes.

Judging the temperature of a charcoal fire

To tell when it's cooking time: Different brands of charcoal burn at different rates; some are ready for cooking sooner than others. In daylight, the coals are ready for cooking when they're covered with a layer of gray ash; at night they'll have a bright red glow. At this stage, spread the briquets into a single layer with tongs and place food on the grill.

Quick temperature test: Hold your hand at the cooking height, palm side down. If you can keep it in position for 2 seconds, the temperature is high or hot; 3 seconds, medium high or hot; 4 seconds, medium; 5 seconds, low.

To lower the temperature, raise the grid, or spread out the coals.

To raise the temperature, tap ash from coals, or push them closer together.

When more coals are needed, add briquets to the outer edge of hot coals.

If spattering fat causes flare-ups, put the flames out by raising the grid, spreading out the coals, or removing a few coals. Have a water bottle handy in case all else fails (remove food before sprinkling). For rotisserie cooking, place a foil drip pan in front of the coals in the firebox to catch the drippings and prevent flare-ups.

Making Cleanup Easy

Keeping the grill clean: Line the grill with heavy-duty aluminum foil. Spray the grill rack with a nonstick coating.

Cleaning the grill if it does get dirty: To remove grease and grilled-on food particles, sprinkle baking soda on a damp sponge and scour; rinse with water/soda solution.

Storing: Clean the grill after each use; then cover it and store it in a clean, dry place.

Barbecue Guide

MEAT	INFORMATION REGARDING CUTS	SERVING INFORMATION	APPROXIMATE DISTANCE FROM HEAT	COOKING TIMES
Beef cubes	1- to 1½-inch cubes of chuck or round, marinated	2 to 3 servings per pound	4 to 5 inches from hot coals	15 to 30 minutes depending on size of cubes, and degree of doneness desired
Beef, ground	Lean	2 to 4 hamburgers per pound, depending on size and thickness	3 to 4 inches from hot coals	10 to 20 minutes, depending on thickness of patties and degree of doneness desired
Beef roasts: tenderloin, rib-eye, boneless rump	Size and shape will vary	½ to ¾ pound per serving for boneless roast	Cook on rotisserie over moderate coals	12 to 20 minutes per pound for medium-rare roast
Beef steaks (tender cuts): club, T-bone, porterhouse, rib, rib-eye, filet mignon	1 to 2 inches thick	½ to ¾ pound per serving for boneless roast	4 to 5 inches from hot coals	20 to 30 minutes for 1-inch-thick, depending on degree of doneness desired; 30 to 45 minutes for 2-inch-thick, depending on degree of doneness desired
Beef steaks (less tender): round, chuck, flank	¾ to 1½ inches thick, marinated	½ pound per serving	5 to 6 inches from moderate coals	20 to 25 minutes, depending on thickness and degree of doneness desired
Chicken (parts)	Halves and pieces	¾ to 1 pound per serving	5 to 6 inches from low to moderate coals	50 minutes to 1 hour
Chicken (whole)	3 to 4 pounds	3 to 4 servings per bird	Cook on rotisserie over moderate coals	1 to 1½ hours, depending on size
Cornish game hens (whole)	½ to 1 pound	1 whole bird per serving	Cook on rotisserie over moderate coals	1 to 1¼ hours

MEAT	INFORMATION REGARDING CUTS	SERVING INFORMATION	APPROXIMATE DISTANCE FROM HEAT	COOKING TIMES
Fish fillets and steaks	¾ to 1 inch thick	2 to 3 servings per pound	4 to 5 inches from moderate coals	10 to 20 minutes, depending on thickness
Fish, whole	2 to 5 pounds dressed	2 to 3 servings per pound	4 to 5 inches from moderate coals	15 to 20 minutes per pound, or until meat flakes easily with fork
Ham: fully cooked, center slice	¾ to 1 inch thick	⅓ pound per serving	5 to 6 inches from low to moderate coals	20 to 25 minutes, turning frequently
Lamb chops: arm, loin, rib	1 to 1½ inches thick	2 chops per serving	5 to 6 inches from low to moderate coals	30 to 40 minutes, depending on thickness
Lamb cubes	1- to 2-inch cubes	2 to 3 servings per pound	4 to 5 inches from low to moderate coals	20 to 30 minutes, turning frequently
Leg of lamb	Boned and rolled	1 pound per serving	Cook on rotisserie over moderate coals	30 to 35 minutes per pound, or until meat thermometer registers 175°
Pork chops: rib, loin, butterfly	1 to 1½ inches thick	1 chop per serving	5 to 6 inches from low to moderate coals	35 to 40 minutes, turning frequently until well done
Pork cubes	1- to 1½-inch cubes	½ pound per serving	5 to 6 inches from low to moderate coals	30 to 40 minutes, turning frequently until well done
Pork roast: boneless leg of pork or loin roast	6 to 11 pounds	⅓ to ½ pound per serving	Cook on rotisserie over moderate coals	25 to 35 minutes per pound, or until meat thermometer registers 170°
Pork steaks: blade, arm	½ to 1 inch thick	1 steak per serving	5 to 6 inches from low to moderate coals	35 to 55 minutes, turning frequently until well done
Ribs: spareribs, loin, back ribs	Cut into serving-size pieces	¾ to 1 pound per serving	6 to 7 inches from low to moderate coals	1 to 1½ hours, turning frequently

Ingredient Substitutions

INGREDIENT AMOUNT	SUBSTITUTIONS
1 tablespoon active dry yeast	1 package active dry yeast, or 1 compressed yeast cake
1 teaspoon baking powder	¼ teaspoon baking soda plus ⅝ teaspoon cream of tartar, or ¼ teaspoon baking soda plus ½ cup buttermilk or fully soured milk, or ¼ teaspoon baking soda plus ½ tablespoon vinegar or lemon juice used with sweet milk to make ½ cup, or ¼ teaspoon baking soda plus ¼ to ½ cup molasses
1 cup butter	1 cup margarine, or ⅞ to 1 cup hydrogenated fat plus ½ teaspoon salt, or ⅞ cup lard plus ½ teaspoon salt
1 cup buttermilk or sour milk	1 tablespoon vinegar or lemon juice plus enough sweet milk to make 1 cup (let stand 5 minutes), or 1¾ teaspoons cream of tartar plus 1 cup sweet milk
1 cup sifted cake flour	1 cup minus 2 tablespoons sifted all-purpose flour
1 ounce chocolate	3 tablespoons cocoa plus 1 tablespoon fat
1 cup corn syrup	1 cup sugar plus ¼ cup liquid*
1 whole egg	2 egg yolks, or 3 tablespoons plus 1 teaspoon thawed frozen egg, or 2 tablespoons plus 2 teaspoons dry whole egg powder plus an equal amount of water
1 egg white	2 tablespoons thawed frozen egg white, or 2 teaspoons dry egg white plus 2 tablespoons water
1 egg yolk	3½ tablespoons thawed frozen egg yolk, or 2 tablespoons dry egg yolk plus 2 teaspoons water
1 tablespoon flour (used as thickener)	½ tablespoon cornstarch, potato starch, rice starch, or arrowroot starch, or 1 tablespoon quick-cooking tapioca
1 cup sifted all-purpose flour	1 cup minus 2 tablespoons sifted all-purpose flour
1 cup honey	1¼ cups sugar plus ¼ cup liquid*
1 cup milk	3 tablespoons sifted regular nonfat dry milk plus 1 cup minus 1 tablespoon water, or ⅓ cup instant nonfat dry milk plus 1 cup minus 1 tablespoon water
1 cup whole milk	1 cup reconstituted nonfat dry milk plus 2½ teaspoons butter or margarine, or ½ cup evaporated milk plus ½ cup water, or ¼ cup sifted dry whole milk powder plus ⅞ cup water

*Use whatever liquid is called for in the recipe.

Equivalent Amounts

Beans, dry, 1 cup	2½ cups cooked beans
Cornmeal, uncooked, 1 cup	4 cups cooked mush
Macaroni, uncooked, 4 cups	10 cups cooked macaroni
Rice, uncooked, 1 cup	3 cups cooked rice
Butter or margarine, 1 pound	2 cups
Butter or margarine, 1 stick	½ cup
Cheese, 1 pound	4½ cups, grated
Chocolate, baking, 1 square	1 ounce
Cocoa, 1 pound	4 cups
Flour, all-purpose, 1 pound	4½ cups, sifted
Macaroni, 1 pound	4 cups, uncooked
Onion, 1 medium	½ cup, chopped
Raisins, seedless, 1 pound	3¼ cups
Shortening, 1 pound	2 cups
Sugar, brown, 1 pound	2¼ cups
Sugar, granulated, 1 pound	2 cups
Sugar, powdered, 1 pound	3½ cups
Walnuts in shells, 1 pound	½ pound, shelled
Basil, dried, ¼ teaspoon	3 teaspoons chopped fresh leaves or 1 small sprig
Celery flakes, 1 teaspoon	2 tablespoons chopped fresh celery
Dill seed, 2 tablespoons	1 head fresh dill
Garlic, instant minced, ⅛ teaspoon	1 clove garlic
Garlic, liquid, 2 teaspoons	1 clove garlic
Garlic powder, ⅛ teaspoon	1 clove garlic
Garlic salt, 1 teaspoon	1 clove garlic
Green bell pepper flakes, 1 tablespoon, plus 2 tablespoons water	2 tablespoons chopped fresh green bell pepper
Horseradish, dehydrated, 1 tablespoon, plus 4 teaspoons water, 1 tablespoon vinegar, and 1/16 tablespoon salt	3 tablespoons prepared horseradish
Lemon peel, grated, bottled, 2 teaspoons	Grated rind of 1 lemon
Marjoram, dried, ½ teaspoon	3 or 4 small fresh leaves
Mint leaves, dried, 1 tablespoon	¼ cup chopped fresh mint
Onion, dried sautéed, 1 teaspoon	1 small onion
Onion, instant minced, 1 teaspoon	1 tablespoon chopped fresh onion
Onion, instant minced, ⅓ cup	1 cup chopped fresh onion
Onion, instant minced, 4 teaspoons	¼ cup chopped fresh onion
Onion, instant minced, ¼ cup	1 medium onion, chopped
Onion, liquid, 1 teaspoon	1 medium onion
Onion flakes, 1 tablespoon	4 teaspoons chopped fresh onion
Onion powder, 1 teaspoon	1 medium onion
Onion salt, 1 teaspoon	3 tablespoons chopped fresh onion
Orange peel, grated, bottled, 1 tablespoon	Grated rind of 1 orange
Oregano, dried, 1 teaspoon	2 teaspoons chopped fresh leaves
Parsley flakes, 1 teaspoon	2 teaspoons minced fresh parsley
Rosemary, dried, ½ teaspoon	2 teaspoons chopped fresh leaves
Vegetable flakes, 1 tablespoon, plus 2 tablespoons water	2 tablespoons chopped fresh vegetables

Equivalent Measures

MEASURE	EQUIVALENT
3 teaspoons	1 tablespoon
2 tablespoons	1 fluid ounce
4 tablespoons	¼ cup
16 tablespoons	1 cup
1 cup	8 fluid ounces
2 cups	1 pint
2 pints	1 quart
4 quarts	1 gallon

Temperature Table

Simmering (at sea level)	180° F.
Boiling (at sea level)	212° F.
Very slow oven	250-275° F.
Slow oven	300-325° F.
Moderate oven	350-375° F.
Hot oven	400-425° F.
Very hot oven	450-475° F.
Extremely hot oven	500-525° F.

Approximate Boiling Temperature of Water at Various Altitudes

ALTITUDE	BOILING POINT OF WATER	
Sea level	212.0° F.	100.0° C.
2,000 feet	208.4° F.	98.4° C.
5,000 feet	203.0° F.	95.0° C.
7,500 feet	198.4° F.	92.4° C.
10,000 feet	194.0° F.	90.0° C.
15,000 feet	185.0° F.	85.0° C.

Steam Pressures at Various Altitudes and Temperatures

TEMPERATURE		SEA LEVEL	4,000 FEET	6,000 FEET	7,500 FEET
228° F.	109° C.	5 pounds	7 pounds	8 pounds	9 pounds
240° F.	115° C.	10 pounds	12 pounds	13 pounds	14 pounds
250° F.	121° C.	15 pounds	17 pounds	18 pounds	19 pounds
259° F.	126° C.	20 pounds	22 pounds	23 pounds	24 pounds

Use this table when adjusting your pressure cooker for cooking at high altitudes.

Spices to Liven Up Any Meal

	APPETIZERS AND SOUPS	MEATS AND POULTRY	EGGS AND CHEESE
Allspice	Split pea or tomato soup; Swedish meatballs	Pot roast; beef stew; sauerbraten; meat loaf; roast pork; raisin sauce for ham	
Aniseed	Cream cheese spread for canapés		
Barbecue seasoning	Tomato juice; cocktail sauce for shrimp; topping for buttered crackers and toast	Hamburgers; meat loaf; broiled or grilled chicken; pot roast; pork chops	Deviled eggs
Basil	Tomato juice; bouillon; vegetable soup	Beef stew; meat loaf; pork chops	Spanish omelet
Bay leaves	Fish chowder; tomato or vegetable soup; minestrone	Corned beef; tongue; beef or lamb stew; spaghetti sauce; pot roast; meat loaf	
Caraway seed	Mix with cream cheese or cottage cheese for dips; split pea soup	Roast pork; lamb stew; meat pies	Cheese sauces; cheese soufflé
Cardamom	Fruit cup	Swedish meatballs; meat loaf; roast pork; barbecue sauce for chicken	
Cayenne pepper	Tomato juice; cheese dips; clam chowder; oyster stew	Barbecue sauce; beef stew; all casseroles	Deviled eggs; egg salad; cheese soufflé; cheese rarebit

FISH AND SEAFOOD	SALADS AND DRESSINGS	VEGETABLES AND FRUITS	DESSERTS
In water for poaching fish or shrimp	French dressings; dressings for fruit salad	Sweet potatoes; winter squash; carrots; beets; cranberry sauce; fruit cup	Fruit pies; custard pie; fruit cake; plum pudding
Poached fish; shrimp; crab	Dressings for fruit salad	Applesauce; baked apples	Pound cake; apple pie; cookies, especially pfeffernuesse
Broiled or grilled fish		Corn-on-the-cob; baked potatoes; baked beans	
Add to lemon juice and brush over broiled fish or shrimp	Sliced tomatoes; French dressing for vegetable salads	Tomatoes prepared in any way; eggplant	
Poached fish	Oil-and-vinegar dressing	Boiled potatoes; creamed or buttered onions; scalloped tomatoes	
Tuna-noodle casserole	Cole slaw; potato salad; cucumbers in sour cream	Sauerkraut; beets; cabbage; turnips; mashed potatoes	
		Baked apples; applesauce; sweet potatoes	Rice pudding; custard; coffee cakes and sweet rolls; gingerbread
Sauces for seafood	Chicken or tuna salad; salad dressings of all kinds	Corn pudding; creamed onions	

	APPETIZERS AND SOUPS	MEATS AND POULTRY	EGGS AND CHEESE
Celery seed	Cheese dips; vegetable or tomato juice; vegetable soup	Creamed chicken; veal or lamb roasts and stews	Cheese sauce; omelets
Chervil	Cream soups	Stuffing for poultry; lamb, veal, or pork roasts or stews	Omelets or scrambled eggs
Chili powder	Guacamole; cheese dips; vegetable soup	Hamburgers; meat loaf; barbecued spareribs	Deviled eggs; scrambled eggs; cheese soufflé
Cinnamon	Fruit punch	Lamb chops or lamb stew; pork chops; ham; stuffing for roast goose	Add to eggs and milk for French toast
Cloves	Borscht; split pea soup	Baked ham; roast pork; beef stew	
Cumin (Cominos)	Bean soup	Meat loaf; chili con carne; baked bean casseroles; pot roast	Deviled eggs
Curry powder	Cheese dips; cream of chicken or mushroom soup	Chicken, lamb, or beef curry; orange glaze for duck or chicken	Creamed or deviled eggs; egg salad
Dill seed	Crush and add to cream cheese for dips	Lamb stew or chops; corned beef	Cottage cheese

FISH AND SEAFOOD	SALADS AND DRESSINGS	VEGETABLES AND FRUITS	DESSERTS
Stuffing for baked fish	Fruit salad dressings; potato salad; cole slaw; chicken; tuna; salmon salad	Scalloped potatoes; stuffed peppers	
Egg sauce for salmon or other fish; stuffing for baked fish	French dressings	Creamed potatoes or carrots	
Seafood cocktail sauce	Dressings for tossed green salad	Spanish rice; scalloped tomatoes; cheese sauce for potatoes, corn, or green beans	
	Fruit salads	Winter squash; sweet potatoes; apples prepared any way; broiled grapefruit	Sprinkle on vanilla ice cream; hot chocolate; bread pudding; baked custard
Sprinkle lightly over baked fish	Fruit salad	Beets; green beans; winter squash; sweet potatoes; creamed onions	Chocolate pudding; fruit desserts of all kinds; especially pears and apples
	Just a pinch in mayonnaise for potato or macaroni salad	Tomato sauces; hot buttered rice	
Tuna-noodle casserole; seafood casseroles of all kinds, especially shrimp or crab	Chicken salad; tuna, shrimp, or crab salad	Creamed vegetables; rice	Hot fruit compote
Poached fish; sauces for salmon and other fish	Cole slaw; potato salad; sliced cucumbers	Cabbage; cauliflower; green beans; sauerkraut; pickled beets	

	APPETIZERS AND SOUPS	MEATS AND POULTRY	EGGS AND CHEESE
Dill weed	Tomato juice; sour cream or cheese dips	Lamb or pork	
Ginger	Bean soup	Beef pot roast; roast pork and lamb; blend with butter and rub into skin of roasting chicken	
Herb seasoning	Tomato or chicken soup; cheese dips	Broiled chicken; lamb chops; veal; marinades for all meats	Omelets and scrambled eggs
Italian seasoning	Vegetable, tomato, or bean soup; sour cream or cheese dip	All Italian dishes; beef stew; meat loaf; lamb or beef casseroles	Tomato sauce for omelets
Mace	Oyster stew; cream of chicken soup	Veal or lamb chops; chicken à la king	Just a dash in Welsh rarebit; creamed eggs; cream cheese; spread for date nut bread
Marjoram	Vegetable soup	Stewed chicken; veal or lamb stews; lamb chops and roasts; poultry stuffing	Cheese soufflé; scrambled eggs
MSG (Monosodium glutamate)	All soups	Meat loaf; stews; casseroles; Oriental dishes; marinades	
Mustard, dry (mix with water, then add to food)	Cream soups; dips; cocktail sauce for shrimp or other seafood	Roast beef hash; meat loaf; cold meats	All dishes using Cheddar or American cheese; deviled eggs
Nutmeg	Chicken soup; cream soups	Creamed chicken; meatballs; broiled chicken	Eggnog

FISH AND SEAFOOD	SALADS AND DRESSINGS	VEGETABLES AND FRUITS	DESSERTS
All fish, especially salmon and shrimp	Seafood salads; potato salad; cucumbers in sour cream	Boiled or mashed potatoes; summer squash or zucchini	
Boiled fish		Beets; carrots; winter squash; honeydew melon; pears	Whipped cream for dessert toppings of all kinds; baked bananas; bread pudding
Poached fish	Any salad dressing; sprinkle over sliced tomatoes or cucumbers	Potatoes; onions; summer squash	
Baked or broiled fish	Add to tossed green salads or any salad dressing	Tomatoes; eggplant; onions; zucchini	
Sauces for fish or fish casseroles	Dressings for fruit salad	Cream sauces for vegetables	Chocolate desserts; pound cake; in biscuit dough and whipped cream for peach or strawberry shortcake
Broiled or baked fish; stuffing or sauces for fish	Chicken and tuna salad	Summer squash; beans; peas; tomatoes	
		Vegetable casseroles; leftover vegetables	
Deviled crab; fish or seafood casseroles; sauces for seafood	All salad dressings; add to commercial mayonnaise	Cream sauces and cheese sauces for vegetables	
Fish cakes; stuffing for baked fish	Dressings for fruit salad	Green beans; carrots; spinach; winter squash; sweet potatoes; add to butter for boiled potatoes; sliced bananas	Apple desserts; custards; add to white or yellow cake mixes

	APPETIZERS AND SOUPS	MEATS AND POULTRY	EGGS AND CHEESE
Oregano	Tomato soup or tomato juice	Spaghetti sauce; meat casseroles; pot roast; beet stew; chili con carne	A pinch in scrambled eggs or omelets
Paprika	Garnish for soups and appetizers	Add to toppings for casseroles and to coating for fried foods; broiled chicken; chicken or veal paprikash	Welsh rarebit
Pepper, seasoned	Soups of all kinds, especially cream soups; cheese dips	Broiled or grilled steaks and hamburgers; lamb or pork chops	Poached or soft-cooked eggs; scrambled eggs and omelets; cottage cheese
Poppy seed	Cheese dips	Add to crust for meat pies; lamb or veal stews; casserole toppings	Scrambled eggs
Poultry seasoning	Chicken soup; liver paté	Chicken casseroles; meat loaf; hamburgers; add to coating for fried chicken; rub on roast pork	
Pumpkin pie spice	Just a dash on cream of chicken soup		Add to eggs and milk for French toast
Rosemary	Chicken, pea, or spinach soup	Stewed chicken; chicken fricassee; poultry stuffing; veal dishes; crush and rub into leg of lamb	
Saffron	Chicken soup; fish soups	Chicken and rice (arroz con pollo); veal fricassee; paella	
Sage	Vegetable soups	Rub on pork roast or chops; poultry stuffings; chicken casseroles; meat loaf; add to pastry or toppings for casseroles	Cottage cheese

FISH AND SEAFOOD	SALADS AND DRESSINGS	VEGETABLES AND FRUITS	DESSERTS
Add to butter for shellfish	Tuna or potato salad	String beans; potatoes; eggplant; onions; tomatoes	
Sprinkle on broiled or baked fish	Livens up color of oil-and-vinegar dressings; garnish for potato or macaroni salad; cole slaw	Sprinkle on creamed vegetables	
Grilled or broiled fish; tuna casseroles	Seafood salads; potato salad; tossed green salad	All vegetables, cooked and raw	
Tuna-noodle casserole	Cole slaw; potato salad; dressings for fruit salad	Buttered noodles; sauerkraut; cabbage	Filling for coffee cakes; add ¼ cup to white cake mix
Stuffing for baked fish; add to coating for fried fish		Creamed onions	
		Winter squash; sweet potatoes; stewed fruits	Cakes and cookies of all kinds; gingerbread; rice pudding
Salmon casseroles; poached fish; stuffing for baked fish	Add to dressing for chicken or potato salad	Summer squash; zucchini; eggplant; cauliflower	
Sauces for fish; fish stews		Rice	
Add to butter for broiled fish		Creamed or boiled onions; boiled potatoes; lima beans; stewed tomatoes	

	APPETIZERS AND SOUPS	MEATS AND POULTRY	EGGS AND CHEESE
Salad seasoning	Sprinkle on raw vegetable relishes	Broiled chicken; hamburgers	Egg salad; deviled eggs
Savory	Bean soup; split pea soup	Pot roast; meat loaf; poultry stuffing; dumplings for stews	Scrambled eggs; deviled eggs
Seafood seasoning	Cream soups; fish chowder; sprinkle on raw vegetable relishes	Chicken dishes of all kinds	Scrambled eggs; creamed eggs
Seasoning salt	Chicken broth; meat soups	Cold roast beef; roast chicken or turkey; hamburgers; steaks; chops	Poached or soft-cooked eggs; deviled eggs
Sesame seed	Dips and canapé spreads	Hamburgers; meatballs; stuffing for poultry or pork chops; casserole toppings	
Tarragon	Tomato or mushroom soup	All chicken dishes; rub into leg of lamb	Creamed eggs
Thyme	Clam chowder; clam dip	Poultry stuffings; lamb or veal stew; chicken fricassee	

FISH AND SEAFOOD	SALADS AND DRESSINGS	VEGETABLES AND FRUITS	DESSERTS
Broiled or sautéed shrimp; broiled or fried fish	All vegetable and meat salads and dressings	All vegetables, cooked or raw; sauces for vegetables	
Baked or broiled fish; fish casseroles		String beans; lima beans; peas	
All fish and seafood dishes	Seafood salads; chicken salad; salad dressings	Use in place of salt on cooked vegetables	
All fish and seafood dishes	All meat and vegetable salads and dressings	French-fried potatoes; sour cream topping for baked potatoes; sliced tomatoes	
Add to coating for fried fish or shrimp	Dressings for fruit salad; sprinkle on tossed green salads	Add to noodles or green beans	Cookies
Add to butter for broiled or sautéed fish and shellfish; tuna casseroles	Tossed green salad; seafood or chicken salad	Spinach; mushrooms; potatoes	
Stuffing for fish; add to coating or butter for fried or broiled fish; lobster thermidor	Chicken salad; dressings for vegetable and seafood salads	Tomatoes; zucchini; peas	

Hints for using spices: If you're unfamiliar with the flavor of a spice or herb, start by using no more than ¼ teaspoon for about 4 servings (except for pepper). More can be added later. Crush leaf herbs to release flavor. Let herbed butters and dips stand for 10 to 15 minutes to develop flavor. Keep spices away from heat and tightly closed. Often, just a sprinkle or dash of spice enlivens flavor.

Appetizers and Dips

Blue Cheese Stuffed Mushrooms

This elegant cocktail hors d'oeuvre is simple to make, requires no cooking, and is as delicious before a summer meal as it is at a party.

NO COOKING   PREPARATION TIME: 20 MINUTES

1 pound medium-sized fresh mushrooms
1 8-ounce package cream cheese,
    softened
½ cup dairy sour cream

2 teaspoons onion powder
2 ounces blue cheese
¼ cup chopped walnuts

1. Rinse and dry mushrooms. Remove stems, and set caps aside. (Stems may be saved for use in soups and stews.)
2. In a medium bowl, combine cream cheese, sour cream, and onion powder and beat until smooth. Press blue cheese through a sieve and stir into cream cheese mixture.
3. Spoon mixture into caps, piling the filling high. Sprinkle caps with chopped walnuts.

MAKES 24 STUFFED MUSHROOMS.

Creamy Herring Salad

From sparkling northern waters to you—a Viking taste delight.

NO COOKING

PREPARATION TIME: 15 MINUTES

1 16-ounce jar pickled herring tidbits, drained and finely chopped
2 apples, peeled, cored, and finely chopped
2 hard-cooked eggs, finely chopped

1 cooked potato, finely chopped
1 small onion, finely chopped
⅓ cup mayonnaise
½ teaspoon ground cinnamon

1. Mix together all ingredients.
2. Serve on crackers or party rye as an appetizer.

MAKES 3½ CUPS.

Deviled Eggs

A picnic necessity, deviled eggs also make an excellent side dish for summer luncheons.

TOP BURNER

PREPARATION TIME: 20 MINUTES

6 eggs
¼ cup mayonnaise
1 teaspoon prepared mustard
½ teaspoon vinegar

¼ teaspoon salt
White pepper to taste
Paprika

1. Hard-boil eggs in lightly salted water, then cool under cold running water for 5 to 10 minutes.
2. Peel shells from eggs and cut eggs in half lengthwise.
3. Remove yolks and mash with remaining ingredients, except paprika, until mixture is smooth. Fill whites with this mixture and sprinkle with paprika.
(For ham deviled eggs, omit salt and add one 2-ounce can of deviled ham to yolk mixture.)

SERVES 4.

Festive Cheese Balls

Rich enough to melt in your mouth—with a surprise in the middle.

OVEN   PREPARATION TIME: 25 MINUTES

1 cup (4 ounces) finely shredded sharp
  Cheddar cheese
¼ cup butter
¾ cup unsifted flour

¼ teaspoon paprika
1 tablespoon water
24 medium-size stuffed olives

1. Mix together cheese, butter, flour, paprika, and water. Form dough into one-inch balls with an olive in the center of each.
2. Bake in 400° oven for 15 minutes. Serve hot.

MAKES 24 BALLS.

Fondue aux Escargots

Most Americans are just finding out why the French consider snails a delicacy. Make converts at your next party with this delicious appetizer.

TOP BURNER   PREPARATION TIME: 25 MINUTES

2 packages containing 12 escargot shells
  each
2 tins containing 12 escargots in brine each
1 cup dry white Burgundy wine

¾ cup soft butter
2 tablespoons finely chopped onion
2 cloves garlic, mashed
2 tablespoons minced parsley

1. Drain all 24 escargots and place each in a shell. Place escargots in a sauté pan.
2. Pour white wine into pan to a depth of one-half inch. Cover, and simmer over low heat until escargots are warm, but do not boil.
3. Combine remaining ingredients in a small pot. Heat until butter is melted and bubbling.
4. Serve fondue style over a warmer. Remove each escargot from its shell and dip it into the sauce before eating.

SERVES 4 to 6.

Italian Stuffed Mushrooms

Try these savory hot hors d'oeuvres at your next cocktail party or to whet your appetite for a full Italian meal.

OVEN   PREPARATION TIME: 45 MINUTES

½ pound large fresh mushrooms
6 tablespoons salad oil
1 cup soft bread crumbs
⅓ cup grated Parmesan cheese

½ teaspoon salt
½ teaspoon onion powder
¼ teaspoon Italian seasoning
1 lightly beaten egg

1. Rinse mushrooms, pat dry, and remove stems, saving stems for later use. Using *four* tablespoons oil, brush outsides of mushroom caps with oil and sprinkle them lightly with salt. Place mushrooms, cavity side up, in a shallow baking pan.
2. Chop stems very finely and mix with bread crumbs, cheese, salt, onion powder, and Italian seasoning. Stir in the egg. Spoon mixture into mushroom caps. Dribble remaining two tablespoons oil over mushroom caps.
3. Preheat oven to 350 degrees and bake mushrooms until hot, about 30 minutes.

MAKES 12 APPETIZERS.

King Crab Dip

A festive dip to impress your most sophisticated guests.

NO COOKING   PREPARATION TIME: 15 MINUTES

1 8-ounce package cream cheese, softened
⅓ cup mayonnaise
1 teaspoon prepared mustard with
   horseradish
1½ tablespoons dried minced onion

½ teaspoon seasoned salt
1 tablespoon chopped parsley
Dash of garlic powder
1 6-ounce package king crab meat, thawed
   and separated into small chunks

1. Blend together cream cheese, mayonnaise, mustard, onion, and salt until smooth.
2. Fold in parsley, garlic powder, and king crab meat. Serve hot or cold.

MAKES ABOUT 1¾ CUPS.

Lobster Cocktail

This appetizer will make you forget that you ever preferred a shrimp cocktail before dinner.

NO COOKING   PREPARATION TIME: 15 MINUTES (PLUS CHILLING TIME)

1 cup cooked, chopped lobster meat
3 tablespoons tomato catsup
3 tablespoons sherry

1½ tablespoons lemon juice
1 tablespoon whole horseradish
¾ teaspoon Tabasco sauce

1. Blend all ingredients except lobster meat. Add lobster meat and mix well.
2. Spoon mixture into four cocktail glasses. Chill thoroughly and serve.

SERVES 4.

Marinated Mushrooms

The clean taste of this appetizer will whet anyone's appetite.

NO COOKING   PREPARATION TIME: 5 MINUTES (PLUS CHILLING TIME)

½ cup Italian dressing
1 4-ounce drained can whole button
  mushrooms

1. Combine dressing and mushrooms in a bowl.
2. Cover and refrigerate one hour. Serve.

SERVES 4.

Mushrooms Stuffed with Crabmeat

Mushrooms rich with the flavor of the Mediterranean –a perfect beginnning for a special dinner.

OVEN   PREPARATION TIME: 35 MINUTES

20 large mushroom caps   2 beaten eggs
Bottled Italian dressing   ¼ cup mayonnaise
1 6-ounce can flaked crabmeat   ¼ cup minced onion
¼ cup soft breadcrumbs   1 teaspoon lemon juice

1. Marinate mushrooms in Italian dressing in refrigerator. Drain.
2. Combine crabmeat, ¼ cup crumbs, eggs, salad dressing, onion, and lemon juice. Fill mushrooms with mixture.
3. Top with remaining crumbs. Bake at 375° for 15 minutes.

MAKES 20 APPETIZERS.

Party Time Meatballs

A platter of these tasty appetizers will get any party off to a good start.

TOP BURNER, BROILER, AND OVEN

PREPARATION TIME: 40 MINUTES

1 pound ground beef
2 tablespoons bread crumbs
1 slightly beaten egg
½ teaspoon salt
½ cup finely chopped onion
½ cup finely chopped green pepper
2 tablespoons butter

½ teaspoon oregano
1 small can tomato soup
2 tablespoons sugar
1 tablespoon vinegar
1 tablespoon Worcestershire sauce
1 teaspoon prepared mustard
Dash hot pepper sauce

1. In a bowl mix beef, bread crumbs, egg and salt. Shape into 40 to 50 small meatballs and place in shallow baking pan. Broil until browned, turning once, and spoon off fat.
2. Melt butter in saucepan while meatballs are browning. Add onion and green pepper and cook in butter until tender.
3. Stir in all remaining ingredients. Pour over meatballs, cover, and bake at 350 degrees for 20 minutes.

MAKES 40 TO 50 COCKTAIL MEATBALLS.

Smoky Cheese Dip

The taste of the great outdoors in a dip that takes only minutes to prepare.

NO COOKING   PREPARATION TIME: 15 MINUTES

1 cup creamed cottage cheese   1 teaspoon vinegar
1 tablespoon milk   ¼ cup (2 ounces) shredded
⅛ teaspoon onion salt   smoke-flavored process cheese food

1. Beat all ingredients together or mix in blender until smooth.
2. Serve with potato or corn chips or on crackers.

MAKES ABOUT 1⅓ CUPS.

Spicy Dijon Escargot

The cold dip for this tempting appetizer may be prepared ahead of time to cut down on those last minute party chores.

TOP BURNER   PREPARATION TIME: 15 MINUTES

2 packages containing 12 escargot shells   1 cup sour cream
   each   2 tablespoons Dijon mustard
2 tins containing 12 escargots in brine each Salt to taste
1 cup dry white Burgundy wine   Few drops Tabasco sauce
1 14-ounce can artichoke bottoms, drained

1. Press artichoke bottoms through a sieve. Mix with sour cream and mustard; add salt and Tabasco to taste. (Sauce may also be prepared by combining all ingredients in blender and blending until smooth.)
2. Chill dip until ready to serve with hot escargots.
3. Drain all 24 escargots and place each in a shell. Place escargots in a sauté pan.
4. Pour white wine into pan to a depth of one-half inch. Cover and simmer over low heat until escargots are warm, but do not boil.

SERVES 4 to 6.

Spinach Dip

Thought you didn't like spinach? Try this dip—it's sure to change your mind.

NO COOKING   PREPARATION TIME: 20 MINUTES

1 cup mayonnaise   2 tablespoons chopped chives
1 cup dairy sour cream   ½ teaspoon salt
1 cup finely chopped raw spinach   Dash pepper
¼ cup chopped parsley

1. Combine all ingredients. Chill.
2. Serve with raw vegetables or Melba rounds.

MAKES 3¼ CUPS.

Zesty Clam Dip

Dip a cracker or chip into this appetizer for a refreshing treat.

NO COOKING   PREPARATION TIME: 10 MINUTES

1 10-ounce can cream of celery soup   1 tablespoon chopped parsley
1 8-ounce package cream cheese, softened   ½ tablespoon chopped chives
1 small can minced clams, well-drained   2 teaspoons horseradish

1. Blend soup into cream cheese with blender or rotary mixer set on slow. Beat until lightly
   blended.
2. Mix in clams, parsley, chives, and horseradish. Chill before serving.

MAKES 2 CUPS.

Soups

Broccoli-Cheddar Soup

Add a glass of wine and a loaf of French bread for a quick and easy hot meal.

TOP BURNER   PREPARATION TIME: 30 MINUTES

2 tablespoons butter
1½ teaspoons instant minced onion
3 tablespoons flour
½ teaspoon salt
⅛ teaspoon pepper
¼ teaspoon celery salt
2 cups milk

2 cups (8 ounces) shredded Cheddar
  cheese
2 chicken bouillon cubes
1½ cups hot water
1 cup cooked chopped broccoli
Dash paprika

1. Melt fat in a three-quart saucepan over low heat. Add onion and cook until lightly browned.
2. Stir in flour and seasonings. Add milk gradually, stirring constantly, and cook until thickened.
3. Add cheese and stir until melted. Remove from heat.
4. Dissolve bouillon cubes in hot water and stir into cheese mixture.
5. Add broccoli and heat to serving temperature. Sprinkle lightly with paprika before serving.

SERVES 4 TO 6.

Chili con Carne

You don't have to go south of the border to try good chili. Just use this recipe.

TOP BURNER   PREPARATION TIME: 50 MINUTES

1½ pounds ground beef   1 1-pound can tomatoes
1 envelope onion soup mix   ½ cup water
2 1-pound cans kidney beans   1 to 2 tablespoons chili powder

1. Brown meat well in a large skillet. Stir in soup mix, kidney beans, tomatoes, water, and chili powder, mixing well.
2. Reduce heat, cover, and simmer for 30 to 40 minutes, stirring occasionally.

SERVES 6.

Creamy Shrimp Soup

This rich soup will quickly warm up any outdoorsman or camper.

TOP BURNER   PREPARATION TIME: 30 MINUTES

2 tablespoons butter   1 envelope chicken soup mix
1 small onion, chopped   1 pound shelled and cleaned shrimp
1 stalk celery, chopped   ¾ cup light cream
4½ cups water

1. Melt butter in medium saucepan, and cook onion and celery until tender.
2. Add water and bring to a boil. Stir in soup mix.
3. Add shrimp and cook two or three minutes until tender.
4. Add cream. Heat to serving temperature, stirring occasionally, but do not boil.

SERVES 4.

French Onion Soup

From the bistros of Paris's Left Bank—a hearty soup to see you through the coldest of days.

TOP BURNER   PREPARATION TIME: 15 MINUTES

1 can condensed onion soup
1¼ cups water
3 thin slices toasted French bread
¾ cup grated Gruyère or Swiss cheese

1. Combine soup and water in a saucepan and heat until just under boiling.
2. Place a slice of French bread in each serving bowl and top with the grated cheese. Pour in the hot soup.

SERVES 2 TO 3.

Nantucket Oyster Stew

This rich, savory oyster stew makes any meal a success.

TOP BURNER   PREPARATION TIME: 15 MINUTES

1½ pints oysters   Salt
2 cups milk   Pepper
2 cups cream   Butter

1. Drain oysters, being careful to remove bits of shell. Reserve oyster liquor.
2. Scald milk and cream. Cook oysters in reserved liquor until edges begin to curl.
3. Stir mixture into milk and cream. Salt and pepper to taste. Spoon into heated soup plates and add a pat of butter to each plate.

SERVES 6.

Old English Cheddar Soup

A hot, hearty winter soup—great with thick slices of buttered pumpernickel bread.

TOP BURNER   PREPARATION TIME: 25 MINUTES

2 tablespoons butter
2 cups sliced onions
1 tablespoon flour
1 quart milk

1½ teaspoons salt
⅛ teaspoon pepper
1 cup (4 ounces) grated sharp Cheddar
   cheese

1. Melt butter in a saucepan. Add onion and cook slowly, stirring constantly, until translucent.
2. Stir in flour. Add 1 cup milk, stirring constantly. Cook until smooth and thickened.
3. Add rest of milk gradually, stirring constantly. Add salt, pepper, and cheese. Heat to serving temperature. Serve immediately.

SERVES 6.

Quick Corn Chowder

TOP BURNER   PREPARATION TIME: 30 MINUTES

3 slices bacon, chopped
3 tablespoons chopped onion
1¼ cups diced potatoes
1 cup water

1 16-ounce can cream-style corn
3 cups milk
½ teaspoon salt

1. Cook bacon in a saucepan until crisp. Remove bacon and save for later use.
2. Add onion to bacon fat and sauté until lightly browned. Add potatoes and water and bring to a boil. Reduce heat, and gently boil for 10 minutes.
3. Add corn and cook over low heat an additional 10 minutes. Stir in milk, salt, and bacon. Bring to serving temperature, but do not boil.

SERVES 6.

Quick Minestrone

Try this shortcut to a hearty, savory Italian favorite.

TOP BURNER   PREPARATION TIME: 30 MINUTES

1 tablespoon olive oil
1 medium zucchini, diced
1 medium tomato, cut up
1 cup chick peas

4 cups water
1 envelope onion soup mix
¼ cup uncooked elbow macaroni
Pinch sweet basil

1. Heat oil in a large saucepan and cook zucchini, tomato, and chick peas for 5 minutes.
2. Add water and bring to a boil. Stir in soup mix, elbow macaroni, and basil.
3. Reduce heat, cover, and simmer for 10 minutes.

SERVES 4.

Spinach and Potato Soup

Full-bodied and flavorful, this soup is perfect for satisfying big midday appetites.

TOP BURNER   PREPARATION TIME: 35 MINUTES

¼ cup chopped onion
2 tablespoons butter
2 cups water
1 teaspoon salt
2 cups diced or finely cut up potatoes

2 cups chopped fresh or frozen spinach
1⅔ cups evaporated milk
1 teaspoon Worcestershire sauce
½ cup shredded cheese

1. Melt butter in a medium saucepan. Add onion, and cook until tender.
2. Add water, salt, potatoes, and spinach. Cook over moderate heat for about 20 minutes until potatoes are tender.
3. Stir in milk and Worcestershire sauce. Heat to serving temperature, but do not boil. Sprinkle cheese on top before serving.

SERVES 4.

Tomato Rice Soup

Delicious homemade soups don't have to be difficult to prepare. Try this recipe for a soup that's as nutritious as it is easy to make.

TOP BURNER

PREPARATION TIME: 30 MINUTES

1 46-ounce can tomato juice
1 large carrot
1 large onion
1 stalk celery

½ cup uncooked rice
3 tablespoons flour
1 tablespoon butter
Salt and pepper to taste

1. Pour juice into large pot. Add whole vegetables and rice. Bring to boil. Cover, reduce heat, and continue to boil gently until vegetables are tender.
2. Melt butter in saucepan. Add flour and lightly brown. Add flour mixture to soup to thicken it. Salt and pepper to taste.

SERVES 6.

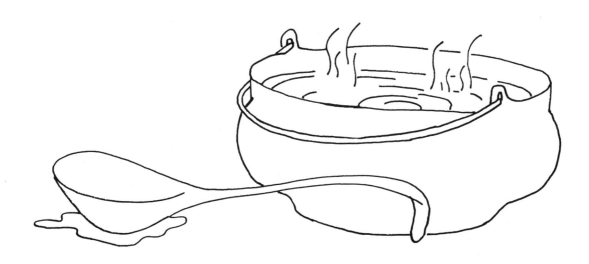

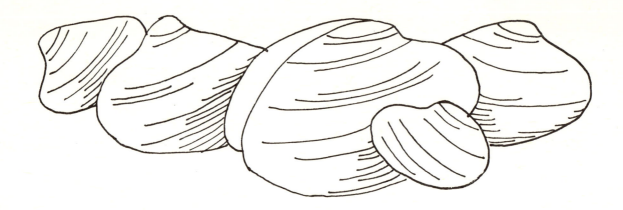

Zuppa di Vongole (Fresh Clam Soup)

The savory ingredients of this classic Italian recipe bring out the full, natural flavor of the clams in a most appetizing fashion.

TOP BURNER

PREPARATION TIME: 30 MINUTES

3 dozen small hardshell clams
4 tablespoons olive oil
1 tablespoon chopped garlic
1 cup dry white wine
2 small cans plum tomatoes

¼ teaspoon oregano
¼ teaspoon basil
¼ teaspoon crushed red pepper (optional)
½ cup finely chopped parsley
1 loaf Italian bread, sliced and toasted

1. Heat oil in a large, deep pot; then add the garlic and cook over moderate heat for just 30 seconds. Pour in the wine, add the coarsely chopped tomatoes, oregano, basil, and red pepper and bring to a boil. Reduce heat and simmer for 10 minutes.
2. Place the thoroughly scrubbed clams, still in their shells, into the sauce. Cover and steam for five to ten minutes, or until the clams open.
3. Ladle the soup into bowls over slices of toasted Italian bread. Sprinkle with parsley and serve.

SERVES 4 TO 6.

Salads

Avocado Chicken Salad

A crisp and lively salad that makes a delicious luncheon.

NO COOKING   PREPARATION TIME: 25 MINUTES

1½ quarts mixed salad greens
½ bunch watercress, shredded
2 cooked chicken breasts, diced
6 slices crisp bacon, crumbled
2 avocados, diced
2 tablespoons lemon juice

1 large tomato, cut up
2 tablespoons chopped chives (or two
  green onions)
1 hard-boiled egg, chopped
3 ounces blue cheese, crumbled
½ cup Italian dressing

1. Combine salad greens and watercress in a large salad bowl. Top with diced chicken and crumbled bacon.
2. Arrange avocado around edge of salad and sprinkle with lemon juice. Top salad with tomato, chives, egg, and cheese. Toss with dressing just before serving.

SERVES 8.

Avocado Crabmeat Salad

A unique combination of tastes and textures, just right for the summer season.

NO COOKING   PREPARATION TIME: 20 MINUTES

½ cup mayonnaise   1 large ripe avocado, peeled and cut up
2 tablespoons lemon or lime juice   1 cup sliced celery
¼ teaspoon salt   1 tablespoon minced onion
2 cups cooked crabmeat chunks

1. Combine mayonnaise, lemon or lime juice, and salt.
2. Gently toss mayonnaise mixture with crabmeat, avocado, celery, and onion.

MAKES ABOUT 4½ CUPS.

Bayou Salad

Make this tantalizing southern favorite for a delightful change from your usual salad.

NO COOKING   PREPARATION TIME: 30 MINUTES

2 6-ounce cans sliced mushrooms   ½ cup salad oil
2 cups halved cherry tomatoes   2 tablespoons wine vinegar
2 cups (1 pound) cooked turkey, cut into   2 tablespoons lemon juice
  chunks   1 teaspoon salt
2 small zucchini, thinly sliced   ½ teaspoon coarsely ground black pepper
1 green pepper, diced   ½ teaspoon sugar
1 scallion, sliced

1. Drain mushrooms. Line a large bowl with lettuce leaves and on them place mushrooms, tomatoes, turkey, zucchini, green pepper, and scallion. Refrigerate until ready to serve.
2. Mix oil, vinegar, lemon juice, salt, pepper, and sugar. Just before serving, pour over salad. Toss gently.

SERVES 6 TO 8.

Caesar Salad

This nutritious, healthful salad is a breeze to make and can be served as a complete lunch or dinner.

NO COOKING   PREPARATION TIME: 15 MINUTES

1 medium head romaine lettuce, shredded   1 tablespoon chopped anchovies
1 cup croutons   Dash pepper
2 tablespoons grated Parmesan cheese   Italian salad dressing
1 hard-boiled egg, sliced

1. Combine lettuce, croutons, cheese, egg, anchovies, and pepper in a large bowl.
2. Toss well and serve.

SERVES 4.

Camper Salad

Prepare this luncheon ahead of time for those days you don't want to be in the kitchen at noon.

TOP BURNER   PREPARATION TIME: 35 MINUTES (PLUS CHILLING TIME)

1 tablespoon salt   ½ teaspoon salt
3 quarts boiling water   ⅛ teaspoon pepper
½ pound elbow macaroni   ½ cup mayonnaise
6 cooked, sliced frankfurters   Salad greens
½ cup diced celery   3 hard-boiled eggs, sliced
½ cup diced green pepper   2 tomatoes, sliced

1. Bring water to rapid boil, add one tablespoon salt, and add macaroni gradually so water continues to boil. Stirring occasionally, cook uncovered for 10 to 12 minutes to desired tenderness. Drain in colander, rinse with cold water, and drain again.
2. Combine macaroni with all ingredients except salad greens, sliced eggs, and sliced tomatoes. Mix well and chill.
3. Serve on salad greens with garnish of sliced eggs and tomatoes.

SERVES 6.

Chicken Luau

A sweet and tangy delicacy from the land of swaying grass skirts and soaring palms.

NO COOKING   PREPARATION TIME: 15 MINUTES (PLUS CHILLING TIME)

2 cups diced cooked chicken
1 13¼-ounce can pineapple tidbits, drained
1 cup sliced celery
½ cup sliced green onion
⅔ cup mayonnaise

2 tablespoons chopped chutney
½ teaspoon grated lime rind
2 tablespoons lime juice
½ teaspoon curry powder
¼ teaspoon salt

1. Toss together first four ingredients. Combine remaining ingredients. Stir into chicken mixture.
2. Chill. Serve on greens.

SERVES 4.

Chilled Macaroni Salad

The macaroni is the only ingredient that needs cooking in this crisp, nutritious salad.

TOP BURNER   PREPARATION TIME: 35 MINUTES (PLUS CHILLING TIME)

1 tablespoon salt
3 quarts boiling water
½ pound elbow macaroni
1 15-ounce can drained red kidney beans
1 cup sour cream
⅓ cup chopped celery
1 cup drained, coarsely chopped sweet
   mixed pickles
¼ cup sweet pickle liquid

2 tablespoons lemon juice
2½ teaspoons prepared horseradish
1 teaspoon salt
1 teaspoon dried chives
½ teaspoon onion salt
Dash pepper
½ pound salami (cut into thin strips)
Salad greens

1. Bring water to rapid boil, add one tablespoon salt, and gradually add macaroni. Stirring frequently, cook uncovered for 10 to 12 minutes to desired tenderness. Drain in colander. Rinse with cold water and drain again.
2. In a large bowl, combine macaroni, beans, sour cream, celery, pickles, pickle liquid, lemon juice, horseradish, and seasonings. Mix thoroughly and chill.
3. Add salami and toss again before serving on salad greens.

SERVES 6.

Confetti Salad

A salad to brighten up any plate—vibrant with the tang of lemon.

NO COOKING   PREPARATION TIME: 20 MINUTES (PLUS CHILLING TIME)

2 cups cooked rice
1 cup diced cooked ham
1 can crushed pineapple, drained
1 banana, diced
⅓ cup chopped celery

⅓ cup mayonnaise
1 teaspoon lemon juice
½ teaspoon ground ginger
Dash salt
Dash pepper

1. Toss together rice, ham, pineapple, banana, and celery.
2. Mix together remaining ingredients. Toss with rice mixture.
3. Pack firmly into one-quart mixing bowl. Chill. Invert and unmold.

SERVES 4.

Crab Salad Supreme

This elegant summer luncheon is best served on a bed of lettuce.

NO COOKING   PREPARATION TIME: 15 MINUTES (PLUS CHILLING TIME)

1 can condensed cream of celery soup
½ cup chili sauce
¼ cup mayonnaise
2 tablespoons minced onion
Dash pepper

1 small green pepper, diced
¼ cup whipped heavy cream
1½ pounds (4 cups) crab meat
1 hard-boiled egg, cut in wedges
2 ripe tomatoes, cut in wedges

1. Blend soup, chili sauce, mayonnaise, onion, green pepper, and pepper in a bowl. Fold in whipped cream.
2. Add the crab meat and mix lightly. Chill for one hour.
3. Serve crab salad on bed of lettuce and garnish with egg and tomato wedges.

SERVES 4.

Creamy Fruit Mold

A colorful warm-weather favorite—use the fruits suggested, or any fruit in season.

TOP BURNER   PREPARATION TIME: 30 MINUTES (PLUS CHILLING TIME)

1 3-ounce package lime- or lemon-flavored
   gelatin
1 cup boiling water
1 cup cold water
1 3-ounce package cream cheese, at room
   temperature

1 cup finely diced apple, unpared
1 cup halved seedless grapes
¼ cup chopped pecans
Several lettuce leaves

1. Dissolve gelatin in boiling water. Add cold water. Chill until thick but not set.
2. Beat cream cheese smooth in small bowl, then add to gelatin and beat with a rotary beater until well blended. Stir in apples, grapes, and pecans.
3. Pour into a one-quart ring mold and chill until firm. Unmold on lettuce.

SERVES 6.

Crisp Shrimp Salad

Here's a tangy shrimp salad that everyone will want to try again.

NO COOKING   PREPARATION TIME: 15 MINUTES (PLUS CHILLING TIME)

¾ pound cooked, cleaned, and cut up
   shrimp
1 tablespoon prepared horseradish
¼ cup French dressing

1 cup sliced celery
½ teaspoon salt
Shredded lettuce

1. Combine shrimp, horseradish, and dressing in a medium bowl and chill.
2. Add celery and salt, toss, and serve on shredded lettuce.

SERVES 4.

Crispy Three-Bean Salad

Chilled overnight, this delightful dish will add just the right accent to any summer luncheon or barbecue.

TOP BURNER   PREPARATION TIME: 35 MINUTES (PLUS CHILLING TIME)

1 9-ounce package frozen cut wax beans
1 20-ounce can chick peas, drained
1 15-ounce can red kidney beans, drained
1 cup chopped celery
3 tablespoons orange- or grapefruit-
   flavored instant breakfast drink

½ teaspoon sugar
½ teaspoon salt
Dash pepper
Dash paprika
2 tablespoons vinegar
¼ cup salad oil

1. Cook wax beans according to directions on package. Drain and cool.
2. Place wax beans, chick peas, kidney beans, and celery in bowl.
3. In a small jar with a tight-fitting lid combine instant breakfast drink, sugar, salt, pepper, and paprika. Add vinegar. Cover and shake until breakfast drink is dissolved. Add salad oil and shake again.
4. Pour salad oil mixture over vegetables and toss lightly. Chill in refrigerator at least three hours or overnight. Serve on lettuce leaves if desired.

SERVES 8.

Deluxe Caesar Salad

The perfect opening course for your next spaghetti dinner.

TOP BURNER   PREPARATION TIME: 20 MINUTES

3 tablespoons butter
½ teaspoon garlic powder
2 cups small soft bread cubes
¼ teaspoon powdered mustard
¼ teaspoon warm water
1 head Romaine lettuce
3 tablespoons olive or salad oil

2 tablespoons lemon juice
¾ teaspoon salt
¼ teaspoon ground black pepper
1 egg
½ cup grated Parmesan cheese
3 anchovy fillets, diced

1. Melt butter in a small skillet. Stir in garlic powder. Add bread cubes and sauté until golden. Set aside.
2. In a cup, combine mustard with water. Let stand for 10 minutes for flavor to develop.
3. Tear lettuce into bite-sized pieces (makes about 3 quarts). Place in a large salad bowl. Combine mustard with oil, lemon juice, salt, and black pepper. Mix well. Pour over lettuce.
4. Break egg into center of salad. Toss well. Add bread cubes, cheese, and anchovies. Toss gently. Serve immediately.

SERVES 8.

Fancy Salad

This is a rich, elegant salad for a luncheon you want to be special.

NO COOKING   PREPARATION TIME: 20 MINUTES (PLUS CHILLING TIME)

4 cups sliced cooked potatoes
1 9-ounce package frozen green beans,
  cooked
½ cup chopped onion
1 cup Italian dressing
3 tomatoes, wedged

Anchovy fillets
Pitted ripe olives
Lettuce
1 7-ounce can flaked tuna, drained
Capers

1. Combine potatoes, beans, onion, and ½ cup dressing and toss lightly. Cover and chill several hours.
2. Add enough additional dressing to potato mixture to moisten and mix lightly.
3. Mound potato mixture in center of platter. Surround with tomatoes, eggs, anchovies, olives, lettuce, and tuna. Sprinkle with capers and serve with additional dressing.

SERVES 6.

Guacamole

Those from the Southwest will need no introduction to this Mexican favorite. Others have a treat coming.

NO COOKING   PREPARATION TIME: 20 MINUTES (PLUS CHILLING TIME)

2 avocados, peeled and mashed
1 cup peeled and cut up tomato
⅓ cup salad dressing
¼ cup chopped onion

1 teaspoon salt
Lettuce
4 slices crisp bacon, crumbled

1. Combine avocados, tomato, salad dressing, onion, and salt. Mix well and chill.
2. Spoon onto lettuce leaves and sprinkle with crumbled bacon.

SERVES 4.

Kidney Bean Salad

The taste and texture of this classic bean salad blend delightfully with the smoky flavor of barbecued meats.

NO COOKING   PREPARATION TIME: 15 MINUTES (PLUS CHILLING TIME)

1 20-ounce can kidney beans, drained   ½ teaspoon salt
¼ cup chopped onion   ⅛ teaspoon pepper
¼ cup pickle relish   ¼ cup mayonnaise
2 hard-cooked eggs, diced

1. Mix together all ingredients. Chill.
2. Serve on lettuce, garnished with parsley and cooked egg slices, if desired.

SERVES 6.

Lobster and Crabmeat Salad

Buy the seafood fresh at a fish market or simply take the top off a can; either way this quick salad will wow last-minute guests.

NO COOKING   PREPARATION TIME: 15 MINUTES

2 cups flaked crabmeat   ½ teaspoon crushed dried tarragon leaves
1 cup cubed lobster meat   ½ teaspoon chili powder
⅓ cup mayonnaise   Dash salt
2 tablespoons chopped tomato   3 large avocados, halved and pitted
1 tablespoon chopped green onion   Pimiento

1. Toss together first eight ingredients.
2. Spoon about a half cup of the seafood mixture into each avocado half. Garnish with strips of pimiento.

SERVES 6.

Lobster Salad

The lobster can be cooked beforehand and chilled or bought pre-cooked to make this elegant, refreshing luncheon dish.

NO COOKING   PREPARATION TIME: 20 MINUTES

2 cold boiled lobsters (1 to 1½ pounds
  each)
¼ cup mayonnaise
¼ cup sour cream
2 tablespoons tarragon vinegar
1 hard-boiled egg, minced

2 small green onions, chopped
¼ teaspoon salt
¼ teaspoon pepper
¼ teaspoon paprika
lemon slices and parsley garnishes

1. Dice lobster meat. Save the shells.
2. Blend mayonnaise, sour cream, tarragon vinegar, egg, green onions, minced parsley, salt, and pepper. Add lobster meat and mix thoroughly.
3. Spoon into cleaned and dried lobster shells (if desired), sprinkle paprika over top, garnish with lemon slices and parsley sprigs, and serve.

SERVES 4.

Macaroni Chicago

The mixture of tastes in this quick salad makes it a Midwestern favorite.

TOP BURNER   PREPARATION TIME: 35 MINUTES

1 tablespoon salt
3 quarts boiling water
½ pound elbow macaroni
1 cup chopped celery
¼ cup finely chopped onion
¼ cup chopped pimiento
1 16-ounce can green peas, drained

2 7-ounce cans flaked tuna, drained
½ teaspoon salt
¼ teaspoon pepper
¾ cup salad dressing or mayonnaise
Salad greens
3 sliced hard-boiled eggs

1. Bring water to rapid boil, add one tablespoon salt, and gradually add macaroni so water continues to boil. Stirring occasionally, cook uncovered for 10 to 12 minutes to desired tenderness. Drain in colander. Rinse with cold water and drain again.
2. In a large bowl, combine macaroni with celery, onion, pimiento, peas, tuna, salt, pepper, and ¼ *cup* of the dressing. Chill, then stir in the remaining dressing. Serve on salad greens with garnish of sliced eggs.

SERVES 6.

Macaroni Salad

A longtime favorite for picnics and cookouts, this versatile salad is also a fine companion for most meals at home.

TOP BURNER   PREPARATION TIME: 30 MINUTES

2 cups cooked, cooled elbow macaroni
¾ cup mayonnaise
⅓ cup sweet pickle relish
2 teaspoons vinegar

6 hard-boiled eggs
2 cups canned pinto or kidney beans, drained
Salt and pepper to taste

1. Cook elbow macaroni according to directions on package. Allow to cool.
2. Combine macaroni and all other ingredients and mix thoroughly.

SERVES 6.

Pineapple Salad Mold

A light, cheery luncheon salad.

TOP BURNER   PREPARATION TIME: 30 MINUTES (PLUS CHILLING TIME)

1 3-ounce package orange-flavored gelatin
1 cup boiling water
¼ cup orange juice
1 cup creamed cottage cheese

¼ cup chopped maraschino cherries
6 canned pineapple slices, drained
6 lettuce leaves

1. Dissolve gelatin in boiling water. Add orange juice. Chill until thick but not set.
2. Stir in cottage cheese and maraschino cherries. Pour into six individual molds. Chill until set.
3. Place a pineapple slice on each lettuce leaf. Unmold gelatin on pineapple slices.

SERVES 6.

Potato Salad

Every cook has his own potato salad secrets. This salad is delicious as is, but also allows you to add your own touches.

TOP BURNER PREPARATION TIME: 20 MINUTES (PLUS CHILLING TIME)

½ cup mayonnaise
1 teaspoon dry mustard
2½ teaspoons salt
2 tablespoons finely chopped onion
2 tablespoons chopped green pepper

¾ cup finely chopped celery
¼ cup sweet pickle relish
1 tablespoon chopped pimiento
6 medium-sized boiled potatoes, diced
3 hard-boiled eggs, chopped

1. Combine all ingredients except potatoes and eggs and mix thoroughly.
2. Pour this mixture over potatoes and mix gently. Add chopped eggs and mix lightly. Chill several hours before serving.

SERVES 6.

Salade Nicoise

This classic salad from the south of France makes an entire luncheon in itself.

NO COOKING   PREPARATION TIME: 45 MINUTES (PLUS CHILLING TIME)

Marinade

1 cup olive oil
½ cup tarragon vinegar
1 teaspoon salt
1 egg yolk

1 tablespoon chopped tarragon
2 teaspoons grated onion
½ clove garlic, mashed

1. Combine all ingredients and beat well.

Salad

1 14-ounce can green beans, drained
1 15-ounce can artichoke bottoms, drained and quartered
2 4-ounce cans tuna fillets, drained
2 hard-boiled eggs, sliced
2 carrots, shredded
1 bunch radishes, sliced
2 tablespoons drained capers

2 tablespoons thinly sliced miniature dill pickles
½ pound Port Salut, St. Paulin, or Bonbel cheese, diced
½ pound fresh mushrooms, sliced
¼ cup pitted chopped olives
1 well-chilled head Boston lettuce

1. Arrange all ingredients, except lettuce, on a large platter.
2. Pour marinade over all ingredients. Chill in refrigerator for several hours.
3. When ready to serve, shred lettuce and arrange on individual salad plates. Allow each guest to choose toppings for lettuce from the salad plate.

SERVES 6.

Shrimp and Asparagus Salad

A classic summer salad with a touch of something different.

TOP BURNER   PREPARATION TIME: 30 MINUTES (PLUS CHILLING TIME)

⅓ cup mayonnaise   ⅛ teaspoon pepper
3 tomatoes, chopped   1 pound cooked shrimp
¼ teaspoon salt   18 cold cooked asparagus spears
½ teaspoon dried basil leaves

1. Mix together first six ingredients. Chill.
2. Arrange asparagus on bed of lettuce, top with shrimp mixture.

SERVES 6.

Shrimp Salad with Fruit

The clean, refreshing taste of fruit with shrimp makes this an ideal summer luncheon.

NO COOKING   PREPARATION TIME: 15 MINUTES (PLUS CHILLING TIME)

2 5-ounce cans cooked shrimp   ½ cup thinly sliced celery
1 20-ounce can pineapple chunks, drained   ¼ cup French dressing
1 cup orange sections, drained   1 bunch endive

1. Mix shrimp, pineapple chunks, orange sections, and celery in a bowl.
2. Add the French dressing and mix lightly. Chill before serving on a bed of endive.

SERVES 6.

Spicy Bean Salad

This quick, crisp salad will perk up any luncheon.

NO COOKING   PREPARATION TIME: 15 MINUTES (PLUS CHILLING TIME)

1 20-ounce can kidney beans, drained   ½ medium-sized green pepper, chopped
1 cup sliced celery   ½ teaspoon chili powder
1 small onion, chopped   ½ cup Italian dressing

1. Toss beans, celery, onions, green pepper, chili powder, and dressing in a medium bowl.
2. Chill and serve.

SERVES 6.

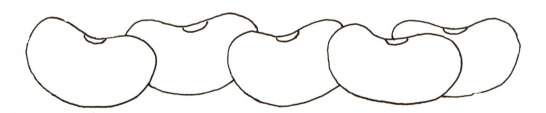

Summer Chicken Salad

Outdoor eating wouldn't be complete without such a crisp, cool salad.

TOP BURNER

PREPARATION TIME: 35 MINUTES (PLUS CHILLING TIME)

1 tablespoon salt
3 quarts boiling water
½ pound elbow macaroni
1 20-ounce can unsweetened pineapple
  chunks
½ cup sour cream
¼ cup mayonnaise
1 teaspoon salt

2 teaspoons dry mustard
½ teaspoon paprika
¼ teaspoon onion salt
2 cups honeydew or cantaloupe melon
  balls
2 cups diced cooked chicken
¼ cup chopped sweet gherkins
½ head crisp lettuce

1. Bring water to rapid boil, add one tablespoon salt, and gradually add macaroni. Boil for 10 to 12 minutes, stirring occasionally, until desired tenderness is reached. Drain in colander. Rinse with cold water and drain again.
2. Drain pineapple, saving ¼ cup juice. In a large bowl blend sour cream, mayonnaise, remaining seasonings, and reserved pineapple juice.
3. Add macaroni, one cup pineapple chunks, melon, chicken, and pickles, and mix thoroughly. Chill. Pour into lettuce lined bowl and garnish with remaining pineapple chunks.

SERVES 6.

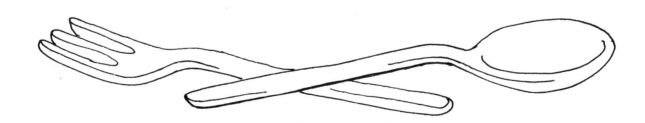

Summer Salad

This main dish luncheon will help everyone keep his "cool" during the hottest days of the year.

NO COOKING   PREPARATION TIME: 30 MINUTES (PLUS CHILLING TIME)

1 head Boston lettuce
1 15-ounce can baby lima beans, drained
3 tomatoes, sliced
2 4-ounce cans tuna (fillets preferred), drained
1 2-pound can white asparagus, drained
⅔ cup olive oil

⅓ cup tarragon vinegar
2 tablespoons drained capers
2 tablespoons finely chopped miniature dill pickles
2 tablespoons finely chopped olives
½ teaspoon salt
1 teaspoon sugar

1. Arrange washed and dried lettuce leaves around the edge of a platter. Spoon lima beans into lettuce leaves.
2. Arrange tomato slices in the center of platter and top with tuna. Place asparagus spears on both sides of tomato slices.
3. Combine all remaining ingredients to make a marinade. Shake in a tightly covered jar until well blended.
4. Pour marinade over salad and chill several hours. Serve cold with French bread.

SERVES 6.

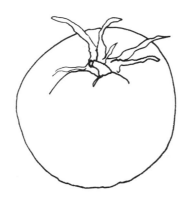

Tomatoes in Marinade

Chilled tomatoes in marinade make a perfect summer side dish.

NO COOKING   PREPARATION TIME: 25 MINUTES

1 envelope Italian or blue cheese salad   3 peeled ripe tomatoes
  dressing mix   ¼ cup minced white onion
Vinegar, water, and salad oil

1. Following directions on envelope, prepare salad dressing with vinegar, water, and salad oil.
2. Slice tomatoes ½ inch thick and place in a shallow bowl or on serving plates.
3. Sprinkle onions over tomatoes, add ½ cup salad dressing, and marinate in refrigerator for two
   hours or more. (Save remaining salad dressing for future use.)

SERVES 4.

Tossed Romaine Salad

*This basic salad, given a delicious twist by the addition of red cabbage, makes a perfect side dish
for any meal.*

NO COOKING   PREPARATION TIME: 10 MINUTES

1 small head romaine lettuce, cut up   1 small onion, thinly sliced
½ small head iceberg lettuce, cut up   6 slices crisp bacon, crumbled
1 cup chopped red cabbage   ½ cup Italian dressing

1. Combine all ingredients except the dressing in a large salad bowl.
2. Add dressing and toss.

SERVES 6.

Tuna Salad

Served in a sandwich or heaped into lettuce cups, classic tuna salad is welcome at any table.

NO COOKING   PREPARATION TIME: 15 MINUTES

2 7-ounce cans tuna, drained and flaked   ½ teaspoon salt
1 cup diced celery   ⅛ teaspoon pepper
Dash lemon juice   ½ cup mayonnaise
1 teaspoon finely chopped onion

1. Lightly mix together tuna, celery, lemon juice, onion, salt, and pepper.
2. Add mayonnaise and serve on lettuce or as a sandwich spread.

SERVES 6.

Tuna Salad Deluxe

Like tuna salad? Try this rich version with delicate herbal overtones.

NO COOKING   PREPARATION TIME: 20 MINUTES (PLUS CHILLING TIME)

2 tablespoons instant minced onion   ½ teaspoon salt
2 tablespoons water   ⅛ teaspoon ground black pepper
⅓ cup mayonnaise   1 7-ounce can tuna, drained and flaked
1 teaspoon lemon juice   3 hard-cooked eggs, chilled and chopped
¾ teaspoon ground marjoram   ½ teaspoon paprika

1. Soak onion in water for 10 minutes. Combine onion with mayonnaise, lemon juice, marjoram, salt, and black pepper. Mix well.
2. In a medium-sized bowl, toss tuna and eggs with mayonnaise mixture. Chill. Just before serving, sprinkle lightly with paprika.

SERVES 4 TO 6.

Tuna Salad with Oranges

This delicious salad can be prepared in advance and kept chilled until mealtime.

TOP BURNER

PREPARATION TIME: 30 MINUTES

1 tablespoon salt
3 quarts boiling water
½ pound elbow macaroni
1 cup sour cream
¼ cup mayonnaise
1 tablespoon chopped chives
1 teaspoon salt

Dash pepper
2 tablespoons lemon juice
1 7-ounce can tuna, drained and flaked
2 medium oranges, peeled and diced
⅓ cup chopped sweet gherkins
⅓ cup dark seedless raisins
Parsley garnish

1. Bring water to rapid boil and add 1 tablespoon salt. Gradually add macaroni to water while it continues to boil. Stirring occasionally, cook uncovered for 10 to 12 minutes to desired tenderness.
2. Drain macaroni in colander. Rinse with cold water and drain again.
3. Combine all remaining ingredients, except parsley, in large bowl. Add macaroni, mix lightly, and chill. Garnish with parsley before serving.

SERVES 6.

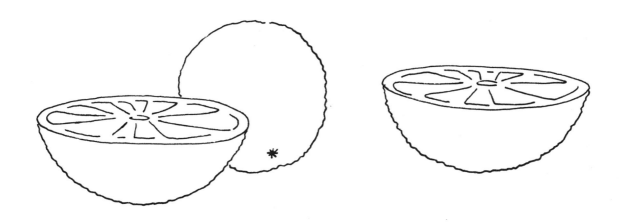

59

Waldorf Salad

A light and cooling dish for a summer night under the stars—and so easy to prepare.

NO COOKING   PREPARATION TIME: 15 MINUTES (PLUS CHILLING TIME)

2 cups diced red apple
½ cup shredded Cheddar cheese
½ cup diced cooked ham
½ cup chopped celery
½ cup chopped nuts

½ cup mayonnaise
2 tablespoons lemon juice
1 teaspoon chopped onion
½ teaspoon salt

Combine all ingredients. Chill.

SERVES 4.

Zesty Potato Salad

For a picnic, barbecue, or just plain lunch, this potato salad is hard to beat.

NO COOKING   PREPARATION TIME: 30 MINUTES (PLUS CHILLING TIME)

⅓ cup French dressing
5 cups cubed cooked potatoes
1 cup mayonnaise
1 cup chopped celery

¼ cup chopped onion
4 hard-boiled eggs, chopped
1 teaspoon salt

1. Pour French dressing over warm potatoes and mix lightly. Cover and refrigerate for two hours.
2. Add remaining ingredients and mix lightly. Chill and serve.

SERVES 6.

Caraway Salad Dressing

This quick salad dressing will be a hit when poured over salad greens, sliced tomatoes, cucumbers, or any combination that strikes your fancy.

NO COOKING   PREPARATION TIME: 15 MINUTES

1 tablespoon instant minced onion
1 tablespoon water
2 teaspoons caraway seed
¾ cup salad oil
½ cup wine vinegar

2 tablespoons parsley flakes
1 teaspoon sugar
1 teaspoon salt
½ teaspoon ground black pepper

1. Combine minced onion and water and let stand 10 minutes.
2. Pour onion mix into container with tight-fitting lid and add all remaining ingredients. Shake well.

MAKES 1½ CUPS.

Thousand Island Dressing

This popular salad dressing is easily made and convenient to have on hand.

NO COOKING   PREPARATION TIME: 10 MINUTES

1 cup mayonnaise
¼ cup sweet pickle relish
2 tablespoons chili sauce

1 tablespoon chopped green pepper
1 tablespoon finely chopped onion
1 hard-boiled egg, finely chopped

1. Mix all ingredients except the egg.
2. Gently mix in the chopped egg. Refrigerate until ready to use.

MAKES ABOUT 2 CUPS.

Sandwiches

Barbecued Hamburger Surprise

Here's one the kids will love.

BARBECUE   PREPARATION TIME: 25 MINUTES

1½ pounds ground beef   2 slices American cheese
12-ounce can mushroom stems and pieces,   6 slices dill pickle
   drained   Hamburger buns
2 teaspoons barbecue spice

1. Lightly combine beef, mushrooms, and barbecue spice. Shape into 12 patties.
2. Cut cheese into 6 strips. Place a piece of cheese and a pickle slice on 6 of the patties. Top with remaining patties. Press edges together.
3. Barbecue over hot coals until done as desired. Serve on toasted buns.

SERVES 6.

Cheese 'n' Chicken on a Bun

A simple, filling meal for a crowd of hungry people.

BARBECUE

3 cups finely chopped cooked chicken
½ cup minced celery
½ cup shredded carrots
¼ cup seedless raisins
⅓ cup mayonnaise

1 teaspoon curry powder
Salt
6 Kaiser rolls or individual hero loaves, split
6 slices American cheese
⅓ cup melted butter

1. In a bowl, mix chicken, celery, carrots, and raisins. Stir in mayonnaise and curry powder. Season to taste with salt.
2. Spread chicken filling on bottom half of rolls. Top with cheese slices. Replace tops of rolls.
3. Brush both sides of sandwich with melted butter. Wrap rolls individually in foil and seal well. Place wrapped sandwiches on grill rack 6 inches above medium-hot coals. Grill 10 minutes. Turn and continue grilling 10 minutes more.
4. Serve with raw relishes and pickles and olives.

SERVES 6.

Denver Sandwiches

These sandwiches are great by themselves, and with a tossed green salad and strawberry shortcake for dessert, they make a superb lunch.

TOP BURNER

PREPARATION TIME: 15 MINUTES

6 slices uncooked bacon, diced
3 tablespoons minced onion
6 beaten eggs
¼ cup milk

¼ teaspoon salt
Pepper to taste
4 tablespoons butter
12 slices bread

1. Partially fry bacon in a skillet. Add minced onion and continue to cook until onion is tender.
2. Mix eggs with milk and seasonings. Pour mixture over bacon and onion and fry on one side until brown. Turn, fry on other side, cut into six pieces, and make sandwiches with your favorite condiments.

MAKES 6 SANDWICHES.

Deviled Ham and Egg Sandwiches

This change of pace will be a welcome addition to any picnic basket.

NO COOKING

PREPARATION TIME: 15 MINUTES

1 teaspoon powdered mustard
1 teaspoon warm water
2 4½-ounce cans deviled ham
4 hard-boiled eggs, chopped

½ cup finely diced carrot
¼ cup parsley flakes
2 tablespoons mayonnaise
12 slices bread

1. Combine powdered mustard and warm water in cup and let stand for 10 minutes.
2. Mix ham, eggs, carrot, parsley, and mayonnaise in a medium bowl. Blend in mustard.
3. Spread over bread to make sandwiches.

MAKES 6 SANDWICHES.

Franks in Batter

Coated with egg batter and fried to a golden brown—hotdogs never tasted better.

TOP BURNER   PREPARATION TIME: 30 MINUTES

½ cup cornmeal   1 beaten egg
½ cup sifted flour   2 tablespoons oil
1 teaspoon salt   12 frankfurters
½ teaspoon pepper   Oil for deep frying
½ cup milk

1. Thoroughly mix cornmeal, flour, salt, and pepper in a bowl. Add milk, egg, and two tablespoons oil, and stir until smooth.
2. Dip each frankfurter into batter, coat thoroughly, and drain excess batter over the bowl.
3. Fry in heated oil for 2 or 3 minutes, turning once, until golden brown. Remove from oil and drain before serving.

SERVES 6.

French-Style Hamburgers

This sophisticated version of the cheeseburger will be popular with gourmets of all ages.

TOP BURNER   PREPARATION TIME: 20 MINUTES

2 pounds lean ground chuck
1 small onion, grated
1 tablespoon Dijon mustard
1 teaspoon salt

¼ teaspoon pepper
1 8-ounce package Bonbel or Port Salut
  cheese
Toasted hamburger buns

1. Combine meat, onion, mustard, salt, and pepper and shape into 12 thin hamburger patties. Using a warm knife, cut the cheese into six round slices.
2. Top six of the patties with the cheese slices. Cover with the remaining patties and pinch edges together.
3. Fry or broil to desired doneness and serve on toasted hamburger buns.

SERVES 6.

Gourmet Ham and Cheese Sandwiches

Served with a tossed green salad, these sandwiches will make lunch a special event.

TOP BURNER   PREPARATION TIME: 15 MINUTES

8 slices white bread
4 thin slices Roquefort cheese
4 thin slices ham

4 thin slices Abbey Port Salut, Bonbel, or St.
  Paulin semi-soft cheese
Butter

1. Fill each sandwich with a slice of Roquefort, ham, and semi-soft cheese.
2. Sauté in butter over low heat, turning once, until each side of sandwich is golden brown and cheese is melted.

SERVES 4.

Gourmet Tuna Sandwiches

Tuna sandwiches will never seem the same after you've tried these.

NO COOKING

PREPARATION TIME: 30 MINUTES

4 cups shredded iceberg lettuce
1 2-ounce can flat anchovy fillets, drained and chopped
3 hard-boiled eggs, chopped
2 tomatoes, diced
½ cucumber, peeled, seeded, and chopped
¼ cup drained capers

6 tablespoons olive oil
3 tablespoons white wine vinegar
1 tablespoon sharp Dijon mustard
1 tablespoon chopped parsley
1 teaspoon crumbled dried tarragon
6 medium hero sandwich loaves
2 8-ounce cans tuna, drained

1. Combine lettuce, anchovies, eggs, tomatoes, cucumber, and capers.
2. Beat together oil, vinegar, mustard, parsley, and tarragon. Stir the mixture into the lettuce mixture.
3. Cut hero loaves in halves lengthwise. Hollow out the bottom of each loaf. Spread with softened butter.
4. Fill bottom halves with lettuce mixture and top with tuna. Cover with top halves of hero loaves and serve.

SERVES 6.

Mushroom Burgers

Tired of plain old hamburger? Try this easy traveling variation.

OVEN OR BARBECUE   PREPARATION TIME: 30 MINUTES

2 pounds ground beef
1 envelope dehydrated onion soup mix
½ cup water
½ cup chopped mushrooms

1. Combine ground beef with soup mix, mushrooms, and water.
2. Shape beef into six patties. Grill or broil until done.

SERVES 6.

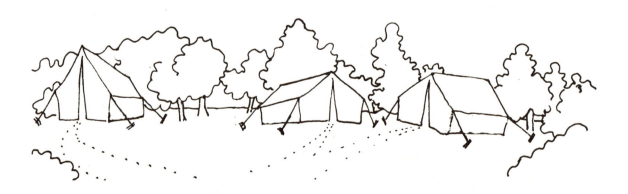

Salisbury Burgers

The bread crumbs, onion, and catsup add a new dimension to these hamburgers.

BROILER   PREPARATION TIME: 30 MINUTES

1½ cups soft bread crumbs   1 teaspoon salt
½ cup minced onion   ¼ teaspoon ground black pepper
⅓ cup catsup   1½ pounds lean ground beef
1 beaten egg

1. Combine bread crumbs, onion, catsup, egg, salt, and black pepper in a large bowl and mix well. Add the beef and mix.
2. Shape into six oval patties about ½ inch thick. Broil 4 to 5 minutes on each side to desired doneness.

SERVES 6.

Teriyaki Burgers

A simple way to add relish to the plain hamburger.

TOP BURNER, BROILER, OR BARBECUE   PREPARATION TIME: 30 MINUTES

2 pounds ground beef
¼ cup teriyaki sauce (see recipe, p.162)
2 tablespoons minced onion
2 tablespoons sweet pickle relish

1. Thoroughly combine all ingredients and make into six patties.
2. Place on grill about three inches from heat (or place in frying pan or on broiler rack) and cook to desired doneness.

MAKES 6 BURGERS.

Picnic Pizzas

Open-air cooking gives a special flavor to these popular snacks.

BARBECUE

1 13¾-ounce package hot roll mix
1 tablespoon salad oil
1 teaspoon crumbled oregano
1 15½-ounce can pizza sauce
½ pound pepperoni, cut into thin round
  slices

1 8-ounce package shredded mozzarella
  cheese
6 tablespoons grated Parmesan cheese

1. Prepare hot roll mix according to directions on package. Knead dough on a lightly floured surface until smooth and elastic. Cut dough into 3 pieces. With oiled fingers, pat each piece of dough into a 9-inch round on a greased piece of heavy-duty aluminum foil. Chill or cover and freeze dough rounds until ready to make pizzas.
2. Place dough on foil on grill rack 8 inches above medium-hot coals. Grill about 5 minutes or until underside of crusts is golden brown. Remove crusts from grill. Remove foil and turn brown side up.
3. Add oil and oregano to pizza sauce. Spread sauce mixture over crusts to within ¾ inch of the edge.
4. Arrange pepperoni evenly on sauce. Sprinkle with mozzarella cheese and Parmesan cheese. Return pizzas to grill rack. Cover loosely with foil dome or hood of the grill. Grill 8 to 10 minutes more or until undersides of pizzas are richly browned and cheese is melted and bubbly.

MAKES 3 9-INCH PIZZAS.

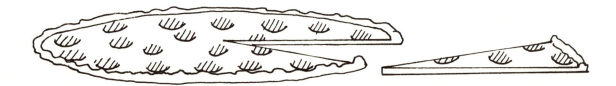

Pasta and Rice

Buttery Linguine

Simplicity itself, but a tasty meal at the same time.

TOP BURNER   PREPARATION TIME: 30 MINUTES

1 pound linguine
½ cup butter
Grated Parmesan cheese
Salt and pepper to taste

1. Cook linguine according to directions on box. Melt butter in small saucepan.
2. Drain linguine and mix lightly with melted butter. Salt and pepper to taste and serve with grated Parmesan cheese.

SERVES 6.

Fettuccine Alfredo

When prepared to perfection, this may be the most elegant of Italy's pasta dishes.

TOP BURNER

PREPARATION TIME: 30 MINUTES

1 tablespoon salt
4 to 6 quarts boiling water
1 pound medium egg noodles
½ pound softened sweet butter

2 cups grated Parmesan cheese
½ cup heavy cream at room temperature
Pepper to taste

1. Add salt to rapidly boiling water. Add noodles gradually so water continues to boil. Stirring occasionally, cook uncovered for 7 to 9 minutes to desired tenderness. Drain in colander.
2. Place softened butter in large heated serving dish. Add noodles and toss gently. Add the cheese and toss again. Pour in the cream and toss gently again. Serve immediately. Pepper to taste.

SERVES 6.

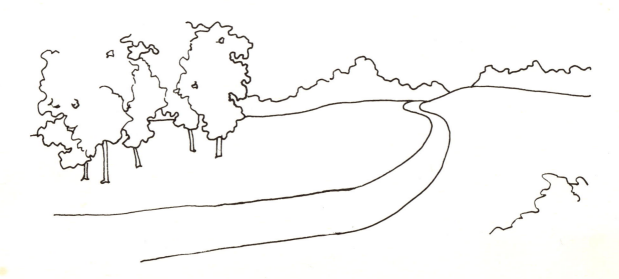

Linguine Bolognese

Bologna is the gastronomic center of Italy, as this recipe will prove.

TOP BURNER   PREPARATION TIME: 1 HOUR

6 slices bacon, diced
2 tablespoons butter
2 cups sliced mushrooms
1 cup chopped onion
½ cup diced celery
½ cup diced carrot
1 pound lean ground beef
1 teaspoon salt

¼ teaspoon nutmeg
Dash pepper
1½ cups beef broth
¼ cup tomato sauce
1 cup dry white wine
¼ cup light cream
1 pound linguine noodles

1. Fry bacon in a large heavy pan until crisp, and pour off all but about one tablespoon of the drippings. Add the butter, mushrooms, onion, celery, and carrot and cook over low heat for a few minutes.
2. Add the beef, stirring to separate meat particles, and brown. Blend in the salt, nutmeg, and pepper. Add the beef broth and tomato sauce. Cover and simmer for 20 minutes.
3. Add the wine. Cover, and simmer an additional 20 minutes. Stir in the cream. (Meanwhile, cook the linguine according to directions on box.)
4. Drain the linguine. Ladle sauce over the noodles and serve.

SERVES 6.

Linguine with Clam Sauce

This Italian classic couldn't be simpler to prepare or more delicious to eat.

TOP BURNER   PREPARATION TIME: 15 MINUTES

1 pound linguine noodles
2 large cloves garlic, mashed
2 tablespoons chopped parsley

¾ teaspoon oregano
½ cup salad oil
2 8-ounce cans minced clams

1. Cook linguine according to directions on package. Meanwhile, heat oil and add garlic, parsley, and oregano. Cook for a few minutes, but do not brown.
2. Add clams with liquid to garlic mixture and simmer about 2 minutes.
3. Serve sauce over drained linguine.

SERVES 4.

Linguine with Garlic

An easy way to prepare either a full meal or a tasty side dish.

TOP BURNER   PREPARATION TIME: 15 MINUTES

3 cloves garlic, mashed
4 tablespoons olive oil
½ pound linguine noodles

Grated Parmesan cheese
Salt and pepper to taste

1. Heat oil in small pan, add garlic, and cook for 10 minutes but do not brown. Cover and keep hot.
2. Cook linguine according to directions on package. Stir 2 tablespoons cooking water into garlic-oil mixture and toss with drained linguine. Serve with grated cheese and season to taste.

SERVES 4.

Spaghetti with Red Clam Sauce

From the sunny shores of Sicily, a pasta dish to wow seafood lovers.

TOP BURNER   PREPARATION TIME: 1 HOUR

2 large cloves garlic, mashed   2 tablespoons chopped parsley
1 teaspoon oregano   ¾ teaspoon salt
¼ cup salad oil   Dash pepper
1 28-ounce can Italian-style tomatoes   1 pound spaghetti or linguine
2 8-ounce cans minced clams

1. Heat oil in deep saucepan. Add garlic and oregano, and cook for a few minutes over low heat. Do not brown. Add tomatoes and cut them into small pieces with the edge of a spoon.
2. Drain the clams and add clam liquid to pot. Add parsley, salt, and pepper. Simmer, uncovered, for 45 minutes, stirring occasionally. Meanwhile, cook spaghetti or linguine according to directions on box.
3. Add clams to the simmering mixture and cook five minutes longer.
4. Serve clam sauce over drained spaghetti or linguine.

SERVES 4 TO 6.

Spaghetti with Sausage Sauce

This spicy Italian dish has become a worldwide favorite.

TOP BURNER   PREPARATION TIME: 2 HOURS

1 pound Italian hot sausage, cut in chunks
¼ cup hot water
1 4-ounce can sliced mushrooms, drained
¾ cup diced carrot
1 medium onion, sliced
½ cup chopped celery
¼ cup chopped parsley
½ pound ground beef
1 28-ounce can whole tomatoes
2 6-ounce cans tomato paste

1 cup dry red wine
1 bay leaf
2 teaspoons salt
1 teaspoon basil leaves
¼ teaspoon pepper
1 tablespoon salt
¼ tablespoon oregano
4 to 6 quarts boiling water
1 pound spaghetti

1. Heat ¼ cup water in a large pan, add sausage, cover tightly, and cook over moderate heat for 10 minutes, stirring occasionally. Remove sausage from the liquid.
2. In the same pan, add mushrooms, carrot, onion, celery, and parsley, and sauté in sausage drippings until tender. Remove from pan. Add the beef to pan and brown it lightly, stirring frequently. Remove any excess fat.
3. Return sausage and vegetables to pan. Add tomatoes, tomato paste, wine, bay leaf, 2 teaspoons salt, basil, pepper, and oregano. Cover and simmer 30 minutes. Uncover and simmer 1 hour, stirring occasionally. Remove bay leaf. (Makes two quarts sauce.)
4. Meanwhile, bring four to six quarts water to rapid boil. Add one tablespoon salt and one tablespoon oil to water. Gradually add spaghetti, and cook uncovered 10 to 14 minutes to desired tenderness, stirring occasionally. Drain in colander. Serve sausage sauce over spaghetti.

SERVES 6.

Chinese Fried Rice

This savory, versatile dish is an excellent way to use up leftover meats.

TOP BURNER

PREPARATION TIME: 25 MINUTES

½ cup scallions
2 tablespoons oil
1 clove garlic
1 cup finely chopped cooked ham, pork,
    chicken, or beef

4 cups cooled cooked rice
2 tablespoons soy sauce
1 egg

1. Dice scallions. Heat oil in a large frying pan and add scallions, garlic, and meat. Stirring constantly, cook over medium heat until onion is tender.
2. Add rice and soy sauce, lower heat, and cook for 10 minutes.
3. Beat egg well, stir into rice mixture, and cook for 5 minutes, stirring constantly.

SERVES 6.

Rice Pilaf

The delicious mixture of tastes will make this one-pot dish a favorite of all the family.

TOP BURNER

PREPARATION TIME: 40 MINUTES

¼ cup butter
2 cups diced cooked ham
1 cup uncooked white rice
2 cups water
¼ cup golden raisins

¼ cup chopped pecans
1 cup chicken broth
⅛ teaspoon dried saffron
⅛ teaspoon cinnamon
⅛ teaspoon ground cloves

1. Heat the butter in a large skillet. Add the ham and rice, and cook until rice is golden brown.
2. Add water, raisins, pecans, chicken broth, saffron, cinnamon, and cloves, mixing well. Bring to a boil. Reduce heat, cover, and simmer for 25 minutes, or until all water is absorbed.

SERVES 4.

Spanish Rice

Robust, outdoor appetites always appreciate the combination of tastes in this filling dish. It's especially good with barbecued meats.

TOP BURNER   PREPARATION TIME: 50 MINUTES

2 16-ounce cans whole tomatoes
¼ cup butter
1½ cups chopped onion
1 medium clove garlic, crushed
¼ cup dry sherry

1 cup long-grain rice
1 chicken bouillon cube
1 10-ounce package frozen peas, thawed
½ cup sliced pimiento-stuffed olives

1. Drain the tomato liquid into a measuring cup, adding enough water to make 1¾ cups of liquid.
2. Melt butter in a saucepan. Add onion and garlic and sauté over medium heat for about 5 minutes or until onion is tender, stirring occasionally.
3. Stir in the tomato liquid, tomatoes, sherry, rice, and bouillon cube and heat to boiling.
4. Cover, reduce heat to low and cook for about 25 minutes, or until rice has absorbed all the liquid.
5. Stir in the thawed peas and olives. Cover, and continue cooking, stirring occasionally, for about 10 minutes or until peas are tender.

SERVES 6.

Eggs and Cheese

Eggs Benedict

Try this simplified recipe to prepare a great brunch.

TOP BURNER

PREPARATION TIME: 35 MINUTES

¼ teaspoon dry mustard
¼ teaspoon water
4 English muffins, split, toasted, and
   buttered
4 thin slices ham
1 envelope hollandaise sauce mix

⅛ teaspoon chervil
4 poached eggs
Seasoning salt
Black pepper
Paprika

1. Combine water and mustard in small pan and let stand 10 minutes. Lightly brown ham in a skillet.
2. Following directions on package, prepare hollandaise sauce mix in pan with mustard mixture. Stir in chervil. Poach eggs.
3. Place slice of ham over 2 muffin halves. Top with an egg. Sprinkle with seasoning salt and pepper, spoon hollandaise sauce over each portion, and sprinkle with paprika.

SERVES 4.

Eggs Fuyung

Broccoli is a nice side dish for this tempting Chinese-inspired meal.

TOP BURNER   PREPARATION TIME: 25 MINUTES

Sauce

1 cup chicken broth (or one cup water and
    one chicken bouillon cube)
2 tablespoons soy sauce

1 tablespoon cornstarch
¼ cup water

Egg mixture

6 eggs
1½ cups diced cooked pork
⅔ cup small, thinly sliced onions
1 16-ounce can bean sprouts, drained

1 4-ounce can mushrooms, drained
2 tablespoons oil

1. Combine broth and soy sauce in a small saucepan and heat to boiling. Blend cornstarch and water and slowly stir into broth. Stirring constantly, cook until thickened. Keep warm while cooking egg mixture.
2. Beat eggs until very thick and light. Fold in the pork, onions, bean sprouts, and mushrooms.
3. Heat oil in a skillet over moderate heat. Pour the egg mixture into the skillet by ½ cupfuls. Cook until lightly browned on one side, then turn and brown the other side.
4. Serve the warm sauce over the patties.

SERVES 6.

Western Omelet Deluxe

Cowboys on the range never had it so good!

TOP BURNER   PREPARATION TIME: 15 MINUTES

4 slightly beaten eggs   Dash pepper
¼ cup mayonnaise   1 tablespoon butter
4 slices bacon, crumbled, or ¼ cup   4 slices toast or 4 English muffins, split and
   cooked diced ham   toasted
2 tablespoons finely chopped parsley   Tomato slices

1. Mix eggs and mayonnaise thoroughly. Add bacon or ham, parsley and pepper.
2. Heat butter in 10-inch frying pan over medium heat. Reduce heat, and pour omelet mixture into frying pan.
3. As edges begin to set, lift slightly with spatula to let uncooked mixture flow underneath. Cook about 4 minutes or until edges are set and top is moist.
4. Roll omelet in pan and cut into quarters. Serve immediately on toast or English muffins with tomato slices.

SERVES 4.

Alpine Fondue

Remember—if you lose your bread cube in the melted cheese, you must kiss your partner at the table.

TOP BURNER AND BARBECUE   PREPARATION TIME: 20 MINUTES

3 cups shredded natural Swiss cheese
1 cup shredded Gruyere cheese
1½ teaspoons flour
1 clove garlic, halved
1 cup Sauternes

1 tablespoon lemon juice
Dash ground nutmeg
Dash pepper
1 loaf French or Italian bread, cut into bite-
    sized pieces with crusts

1. Combine cheeses and flour. Rub inside of heavy saucepan with garlic and discard garlic. Pour in Sauternes and lemon juice.
2. Heat to just under boiling. (Stir constantly and vigorously from here on.)
3. Add a handful of cheese mixture, keeping heat medium. Do not boil. When melted, add more cheese.
4. After all cheese is blended and bubbling, add nutmeg and pepper. Place saucepan on grill over hot coals to keep warm. If fondue becomes too thick, stir in a little warmed Sauternes.
5. Spear bread cube with fork. Dip into fondue and swirl to coat.

SERVES 4 TO 6.

Cheese and Fruit Combinations

Cheese and fruit makes a quick and easy lunch on-the-go. Be sure to dip cut apples and pears in lemon or other citrus juices to keep them from darkening.

Cheese	Fruit
Blue or Roquefort	Apples or pears, especially Anjou and Bosc pears
Brick	Tokay grapes
Camembert	Apples, pears, or tart plums
Cheddar	Tart apples or melon slices
Edam or Gouda	Apples, orange sections, or pineapple spears
Muenster or Swiss	Apples, seedless grapes, or orange sections
Provolone	Sweet Bartlett pears

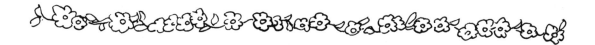

Creamy Rarebit

For cheese lovers—a lunch that really sticks to your ribs.

TOP BURNER   PREPARATION TIME: 25 MINUTES

3 cups (12 ounces) shredded sharp
   Cheddar cheese
1¼ cups milk
1 beaten egg

1 teaspoon Worcestershire sauce
½ teaspoon dry mustard
2 tablespoons chopped pimiento
6 slices toast

1. Combine all ingredients except for pimiento and toast. Cook over low heat, stirring constantly, until cheese melts and mixture is slightly thickened.
2. Stir in pimiento and serve immediately on toast.

SERVES 6.

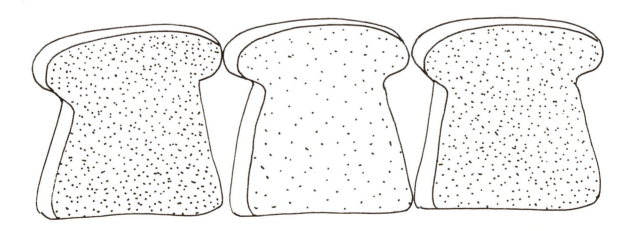

Mountain Cheese Fondue

Fondues are fun, and this one, made with fine cheeses from the mountains of France, is fantastic.

TOP BURNER   PREPARATION TIME: 30 MINUTES

3 pounds grated Comte, Cantal or Gruyere
   cheese
⅔ cup flour
½ clove garlic

6 cups dry white wine
⅔ cup Armagnac
Salt and pepper to taste
Bite-sized pieces of French bread

1. Mix the cheese and flour in a bowl. Rub an earthenware or pyrex pot with garlic. Pour wine into pot and heat until wine begins to bubble.
2. Add cheese mixture to wine one handful at a time, stirring well until fondue is smooth.
3. Stir in Armagnac, and salt and pepper to taste.
4. Place pot over warmer, spear bread on fondue fork, and dip into fondue.

SERVES 12.

Quiche Lorraine

This custardy pie will be the main attraction of a very special meal.

OVEN   PREPARATION TIME: 1 HOUR

8 ounces bacon
1 unbaked 9-inch pastry shell
1½ cups (7 ounces) coarsely shredded
   natural Swiss cheese
¾ teaspoon salt

¼ teaspoon pepper
Dash cayenne
Dash nutmeg
4 eggs
1½ cups half-and-half

1. Cut bacon into pieces and fry until brown and very crisp. Drain well.
2. Crumble bacon into pastry shell. Sprinkle cheese over bacon. Mix seasonings and sprinkle over cheese.
3. Beat eggs and half-and-half together. Pour over cheese and bacon. Bake in 375° oven for 45 minutes or until lightly browned and a knife inserted into the center comes out clean.

SERVES 6.

Seafood

Buttery Steamed Clams

Steamed clams are simple to prepare and a seafood favorite on both coasts.

TOP BURNER

PREPARATION TIME: 30 MINUTES

8 dozen long neck, steamer, or soft-shell clams
4 tablespoons butter (plus ½ pound melted butter)

½ cup finely chopped onions
2 tablespoons chopped fresh parsley
3 cups water

1. Wash clams thoroughly, discarding any with broken shells.
2. Melt four tablespoons butter in a large pot over moderate heat. Add the onions and cook for about 5 minutes, stirring frequently. Stir in the parsley and water and bring to a boil over high heat.
3. Add the clams, cover pot tightly, and steam for 5 to 8 minutes, shaking the pot occasionally. Clams are ready when the shells open. (Discard any clams whose shells do not open.)
4. Remove the clams to a serving bowl. Strain the broth remaining through a fine sieve (or a paper coffee filter) into four or six cups. Serve the melted butter in separate cups.
5. Remove clam from shell, dip it into the broth to remove any traces of sand, and dip it in the melted butter before eating.

SERVES 4 TO 6.

Edgartown Clam Chowder

A full, rich chowder that has been a New England favorite for years and years.

TOP BURNER   PREPARATION TIME: 30 MINUTES

3 quarts hard clams   1 cup diced potatoes
¼ cup diced salt pork   ½ teaspoon salt
¼ cup chopped onion   Dash pepper
1 cup clam liquor and water   2 cups milk

1. Shuck the clams, being careful to remove bits of shell, and chop them.
2. Fry salt pork until golden. Add the onion and cook until onions are transparent.
3. Add the clam liquor, potatoes, seasonings, and clams. Cook over moderate heat about 15 minutes until potatoes are tender.
4. Add the milk very slowly, stirring constantly. Heat to serving temperature, but do not boil. Serve with crackers.

SERVES 4.

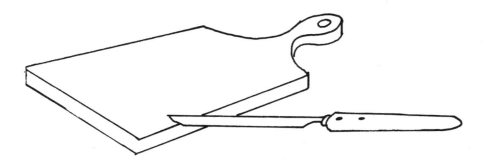

Fried Clams

Here is one of the simplest and, many say, one of the most delicious ways to prepare this delectable shellfish.

TOP BURNER

PREPARATION TIME: 25 MINUTES

1 quart shucked steamer clams
1 beaten egg
1 tablespoon milk

1 teaspoon salt
Dash pepper
1 cup dry bread crumbs

1. Drain the clams and wipe them dry. Combine the egg, milk, and seasonings in a bowl. Dip the clams in the egg mixture and roll them in the bread crumbs until well coated.
2. Fry the clams in a basket in deep fat (at about 375°) until golden brown (about 3 minutes).
3. Drain the clams on paper towels and serve plain, sprinkled with salt, or with tartar sauce.

SERVES 4.

Grilled Soft-Shell Crabs

If you like steamed crabs, you'll love these—grilled and basted in a delicately seasoned sauce.

BARBECUE

PREPARATION TIME: 25 MINUTES

12 fresh or frozen dressed soft-shell blue
   crabs
¾ cup chopped parsley
½ cup oil
1 teaspoon lemon juice

¼ teaspoon nutmeg
¼ teaspoon soy sauce
Dash Tabasco sauce
Lemon wedges

1. Thaw if frozen, and clean, wash, and dry crabs. Place crabs in well-greased, hinged wire grills.
2. In a saucepan, combine all remaining ingredients, except lemon wedges, and heat. Baste crabs with heated sauce.
3. Place crabs about 4 inches from moderately hot coals and cook for 8 minutes. Baste with sauce.
4. Turn and cook another 7 to 10 minutes or until lightly browned. Serve with lemon wedges.

SERVES 6.

Chinese Lobster

Pork and lobster? This one-pot dish will convince you they go together like love and marriage.

TOP BURNER   PREPARATION TIME: 30 MINUTES

½ pound ground pork
2 medium cloves garlic, minced
¼ cup vegetable oil
1½ pounds raw lobster, cut in small pieces
1 can condensed chicken broth
1 cup water

½ cup sliced green onions
2 tablespoons soy sauce
Pepper to taste
3 tablespoons cornstarch
¼ cup water
1 slightly beaten egg

1. In a large skillet, heat oil. Add pork and garlic and cook over moderate heat until pork is cooked thoroughly.
2. Add lobster, soup, water, onions, soy sauce, and pepper. Cook over low heat for 2 or 3 minutes or until lobster is done.
3. Mix cornstarch and ¼ cup water in a small bowl and gradually add to sauce in skillet. Cook, stirring until thickened. Stir egg into sauce and mix lightly.

SERVES 6.

Lobster Stew

Perfect lobster stew is a gourmet's delight, but perfection doesn't allow for shortcuts. Remember that aging for at least five to six hours is necessary to bring out full flavor.

TOP BURNER   PREPARATION TIME: 40 MINUTES (PLUS AGING)

4 1-pound lobsters   1 quart milk
½ cup butter   Salt and pepper to taste

1. Boil 3 quarts of water. Add 2 tablespoons salt. Place lobsters in water and boil for 20 minutes. Remove the meat immediately and save coral and tomalley if desired. Cut meat into large chunks.
2. In a heavy, deep pot, simmer coral and tomalley in ½ cup butter for 7 or 8 minutes. Add the lobster meat and cook over low heat for 10 minutes. Remove from heat and let cool slightly.
3. Heat 1 quart milk, but do not boil. Stirring constantly, add the hot milk—a mere trickle at a time—to the lobster. Salt and pepper to taste.
4. Let lobster stew stand in a cool place for two hours, then refrigerate. Stew should be aged a minimum of 5 to 6 hours. Reheat before serving.

SERVES 4.

Tangy Lobster

Use leftover or canned lobster to make this special luncheon dish.

TOP BURNER   PREPARATION TIME: 20 MINUTES

⅓ cup butter   Pepper to taste
1 teaspoon Worcestershire sauce   2 cups cooked or canned lobster meat,
1 tablespoon lemon juice   cut up
1 teaspoon dry mustard   4 slices toast
½ teaspoon salt

1. Melt butter in top of double boiler. Stir in Worcestershire sauce, lemon juice, mustard, salt, and pepper.
2. Add lobster to mixture and cook about 6 minutes, or until heated through. Serve on toast with lemon wedges.

SERVES 4.

Mussels in Marinade

"Poor man's oysters," as mussels sometimes have been called, can be elegantly served by arranging on a platter six large leaves of lettuce, each filled with potato salad, and topped with the mussels and a garnish of sliced black olives.

TOP BURNER   PREPARATION TIME: 30 MINUTES

Mussels

3 dozen fresh mussels
2½ cups dry white wine
5 chopped shallots
4 sprigs parsley

Marinade

½ cup olive oil   ½ teaspoon pepper
1 tablespoon lemon juice   1 tablespoon shallots
½ teaspoon salt   ½ cup Italian parsley

1. Clean and scrub the mussels and place them in a large pot—without layering, if possible. Cover with the white wine and add shallots and parsley.
2. Cover and cook over high heat, agitating the pot occasionally, for 10 to 12 minutes. The mussels are cooked when their shells open. Then drain the mussels and remove the shells.
3. Make the marinade by thoroughly mixing the olive oil, lemon juice, salt, and pepper. Gently mix the mussels into the marinade. Add the shallots and parsley.
4. Cover, chill, and serve cold.

SERVES 6.

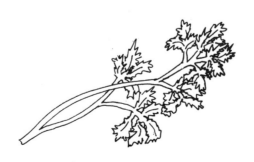

New Bedford Scallops

Scallops and spinach make a one-dish meal.

TOP BURNER AND BROILER   PREPARATION TIME: 25 MINUTES

½ cup butter
½ cup minced raw spinach
2 tablespoons minced onion
4 tablespoons minced lettuce
2 tablespoons minced celery

4 tablespoons fine dry bread crumbs
½ teaspoon anchovy paste
Pepper
¼ teaspoon salt
3 pounds large sea scallops

1. Melt 5 tablespoons of butter in a saucepan. Add all remaining ingredients except for scallops and mix well. Warm the mixture over low heat, but do not let butter brown.
2. Place scallops on a foil-lined broiler pan, dot with remaining butter, and broil until lightly browned.
3. Bunch scallops on serving plate, spread spinach mixture over all, and reheat in broiler until thoroughly heated.

SERVES 6.

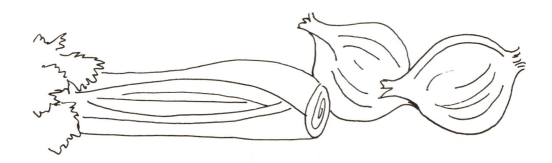

Portuguese Scallops

The delicate flavor of scallops is enhanced by light seasoning.

TOP BURNER   PREPARATION TIME: 15 MINUTES

1 pound sea scallops   ½ teaspoon salt
¼ cup butter or margarine   Dash pepper
1 clove garlic, minced   ½ cup chopped parsley

1. Cut scallops in half. Pat dry with paper towels.
2. Melt butter or margarine in a skillet. Add garlic and salt. Cook until garlic is golden brown.
3. Add scallops. Cook 5 to 7 minutes stirring frequently. Sprinkle with pepper.
4. Add parsley. Cook 1 minute longer. Serve hot.

SERVES 8.

Scallops Provençale

Try this recipe from southern France for delicious scallops in record time.

TOP BURNER   PREPARATION TIME: 20 MINUTES

1½ pounds fresh or defrosted scallops   2 cloves garlic, minced
Seasoned flour   ½ cup chopped parsley
6 tablespoons olive oil   Salt and pepper to taste

1. Dust scallops with seasoned flour. Heat oil in a skillet.
2. Add scallops and garlic. Cook quickly over high heat, tossing scallops to make them brown evenly. Salt and pepper to taste.
3. Remove from heat and gently mix scallops with parsley to coat evenly.

SERVES 4.

Fantail Shrimp

Garnished with lemon wedges, fantail shrimp are as attractive as they are tasty.

1 pound large raw shrimp
2 eggs
1½ teaspoons sugar
½ teaspoon salt

¼ teaspoon pepper
¼ cup flour
2 cups salad oil
Lemon wedges

1. Wash, shell, and devein shrimp, leaving tails on. Cut a slit starting about ½ inch from head end and running to within about ½ inch of tail. Pull tail through slit to make a butterflied, fantail shape.
2. Beat eggs slightly and add sugar, salt, pepper, and flour, and mix well.
3. Dip shrimp in egg mixture. Cook in deep fat until golden brown (about 3 minutes on each side). Serve hot.

SERVES 4.

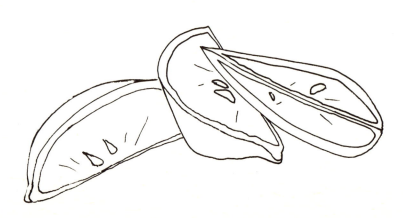

Shrimp Creole

This savory dish, served over a mound of white rice, has been a Louisiana favorite for generations.

TOP BURNER

PREPARATION TIME: 60 MINUTES

2 pounds canned peeled tomatoes
3 pounds uncooked medium-sized shrimp
½ cup vegetable oil
2 cups diced onions
1 cup diced green peppers
1 cup chopped celery
2 teaspoons minced garlic
1 cup water

2 bay leaves
1 tablespoon paprika
½ teaspoon cayenne pepper
1 tablespoon salt
2 tablespoons cornstarch mixed with ¼ cup cold water
8 cups cooked white rice

1. Coarsely chop tomatoes and drain thoroughly. Shell and devein shrimp. Wash them under cold water and drain on paper towels.
2. Heat the oil over moderate heat in a 4- to 6-quart casserole. Add onions, green peppers, celery, and garlic. Cook for about 5 minutes, stirring frequently, until the vegetables are soft.
3. Add the tomatoes, water, bay leaves, paprika, cayenne, and salt. Stir, and bring to a boil over high heat. Partially cover the casserole, reduce heat to low, and stir occasionally. Simmer for 20 to 25 minutes or until mixture thickens. Add shrimp and continue to simmer for another 5 minutes or until shrimp are pink and firm.
4. Mix cornstarch and water and stir until smooth. Pour mixture into casserole. Stir over low heat for 2 to 3 minutes until sauce thickens slightly. Discard bay leaves.
5. Serve hot from the casserole or ladle over mounds of cooked white rice.

SERVES 6.

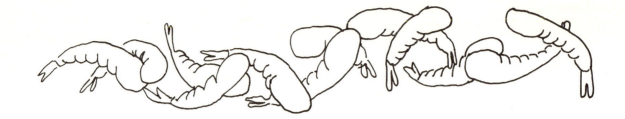

Shrimp Provençale

Well flavored with garlic and herbs, this robust dish is a tradition in Provence, that beautiful and romantic region of France.

TOP BURNER   PREPARATION TIME: 30 MINUTES

2 pounds extra large raw shrimp
½ cup milk
½ cup flour
½ cup oil
2 tablespoons butter

2 or 3 cloves garlic, minced
2 large tomatoes, peeled, seeded, and
   chunked
1 tablespoon chopped parsley
1 lemon

1. Shell, clean, devein, and butterfly shrimp by slicing three quarters of the way down their backs. Heat a small amount of the oil in a large skillet.
2. Dip shrimp into milk, then coat with flour. Sauté in oil over high heat until shrimp begin to turn brown. Then cook over medium heat for 5 minutes. Place cooked shrimp on serving platter and keep warm. Repeat operation until all shrimp is cooked.
3. Melt the butter in a small skillet. Stir in garlic, tomatoes, parsley, and juice of ½ lemon. Pour over shrimp, garnish with lemon wedges, and serve immediately.

SERVES 4 TO 6.

Barbecued Fish Kabobs

You can prepare the night before to make this special barbecue treat.

BARBECUE

PREPARATION TIME: 20 MINUTES

4 cloves garlic, crushed
1 teaspoon crushed red peppers
1 teaspoon paprika
1 tablespoon salt

1 cup wine vinegar
2 cups water
2 crushed bay leaves
4 to 5 pounds cod or haddock fillets

1. To make "vinha de alhos" marinade, combine all ingredients except the fish. Pour marinade over fillets, and let stand overnight.
2. Drain the fish and save the marinade. Cut fillets in long, 1-inch wide strips. Wind fish strips on skewers, making loops in opposite directions and running skewer through each loop.
3. Broil on barbecue grill about 4 inches above hot coals for about 15 minutes, or until fish flakes easily. Turn fish skewers often and brush with marinade. Serve on frankfurter rolls that have been heated on grill.

SERVES 8.

Barbecued Snapper Steaks

A few hickory chips added to your barbecue coals will give this tasty fish an added smoky flavor.

BARBECUE

PREPARATION TIME: 25 MINUTES

2 pounds fresh or frozen red snapper steaks
½ cup oil
¼ cup lemon juice
2 teaspoons salt

½ teaspoon Worcestershire sauce
¼ teaspoon white pepper
Dash Tabasco sauce
Paprika

1. Thaw fish steaks if frozen and cut into serving-sized portions. Place fish in well-greased hinged wire grills.
2. In a bowl, combine all remaining ingredients, except paprika, and mix well. Baste fish with sauce on both sides and sprinkle with paprika.
3. Place fish about 4 inches above moderately hot coals and cook for 8 minutes. Baste with sauce and sprinkle with paprika.
4. Turn and cook another 7 to 10 minutes or until fish flakes easily with a fork.

SERVES 6.

Cranberry and Peach Fish Sticks

Don't snicker. Just try it; you'll like it.

OVEN   PREPARATION TIME: 30 MINUTES

3 packages breaded frozen fish sticks   6 canned cling peaches, halved
½ cup melted butter   ½ cup canned cranberry sauce

1. Defrost fish sticks completely, brush all sides with melted butter, and arrange on a baking sheet.
2. Bake at 425° for 15 minutes or until fish flakes easily with a fork.
3. Brush cut surfaces of peach halves with melted butter and broil 4 inches below heat until peaches begin to brown.
4. Fill peach hollows with cranberry sauce. Arrange on platter with fish sticks and garnish with parsley.

SERVES 6.

Creamy Fish Chablis

A rich and creamy dish whose texture you'll find as delightful as its taste.

TOP BURNER AND OVEN   PREPARATION TIME: 35 MINUTES

1½ pounds fillet of sole or flounder   ½ cup dry white wine (Chablis preferred)
1 cup sliced mushrooms   1 10-ounce can condensed cream of celery
2 tablespoons finely chopped onion   soup
2 tablespoons chopped parsley   ¼ cup whipped heavy cream

1. Place fish fillets in a skillet and top with mushrooms, onion, and parsley. Add the wine, cover, and cook over a low heat for 10 minutes.
2. Transfer fish and garnish to an oven-proof platter. Stir the celery soup into ¼ cup of the remaining liquid and heat. Fold in the whipped cream and pour over fish.
3. Broil until lightly browned.

SERVES 6.

Deviled Scrod

This spicy delicacy is guaranteed to tempt even the most jaded appetites.

BROILER   PREPARATION TIME: 30 MINUTES

1½ to 2 pounds scrod (haddock or cod may   ⅛ teaspoon Tabasco sauce
   be substituted)   3½ tablespoons lemon juice
¼ cup chopped green pepper   ½ cup butter
¼ cup minced onion   2 cups soft bread crumbs
1 tablespoon prepared mustard   2 tablespoons grated Parmesan cheese
1 teaspoon Worcestershire sauce

1. Wipe scrod with a damp cloth and cut into 4 portions.
2. Combine green pepper, onion, mustard, Worcestershire sauce, Tabasco, and lemon juice in bowl. Melt butter and stir in bread crumbs. Blend well with vegetable mixture.
3. Season scrod with salt and pepper, dot with butter or margarine, and place on foil-lined broiler rack about 4 inches below heat for 5 minutes.
4. Remove from broiler, turn scrod, and top with bread and vegetable mixture.
5. Return to broiler for 5 to 7 minutes or until scrod flakes easily with a fork. Sprinkle with Parmesan cheese and broil 1 minute more.

SERVES 4.

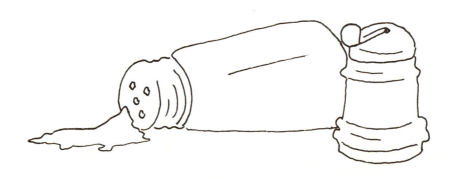

Fish à la Japonaise

The piquant marinade adds a delicate flavor to the simplest fish dish.

OVEN OR TOP BURNER   PREPARATION TIME: 40 MINUTES

¼ cup soy sauce
½ cup sherry
1½ tablespoons salad oil

1 tablespoon finely chopped green onion
2 pounds fish fillets or steaks
1 can mandarin orange slices

1. Combine soy sauce with wine, salad oil, and onion. Let stand 20 minutes to blend flavors.
2. Marinate fish for 10 to 15 minutes. Bake, broil, or pan fry as usual.
3. Garnish with a few orange sections just before serving.

SERVES 4.

Fish with Orange Sauce

A quick and easy way to add fruity excitement to frozen fish.

OVEN   PREPARATION TIME: 35 MINUTES

2 packages breaded frozen fish (8 portions)
¼ cup orange juice
1 tablespoon grated orange peel

⅓ cup melted butter
1 teaspoon lemon juice
dash mace

1. Thaw fish and place in shallow greased baking pan.
2. Combine all other ingredients and pour evenly over fish.
3. Bake fish at 350° for 25 minutes or until fish flakes easily with a fork.
4. Arrange fish on platter and pour any remaining sauce over portions. Garnish with orange slices and parsley.

SERVES 4 TO 6.

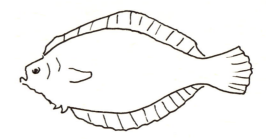

Flounder in a Boat

You can prepare these fillets ahead of time and keep them chilled until the grill is lighted.

BARBECUE

PREPARATION TIME: 40 MINUTES

6 flounder fillets (fresh or frozen and
   thawed)
Salt
Pepper
1 4-ounce jar pimiento, drained and
   chopped

¼ pound trimmed and chopped
   mushrooms
3 tablespoons chopped chives or scallions
¼ cup finely chopped parsley
6 tablespoons melted butter or margarine
6 tablespoons white wine

1. Place flounder fillets on 6 pieces of heavy-duty aluminum foil. Sprinkle each fillet with salt, pepper, pimiento, mushrooms, chives, and parsley.
2. Place 1 tablespoon butter and 1 tablespoon wine on each fillet. Bunch foil up and around the fillets and shape into 6 bundles. Place bundles 8 inches above medium-hot coals and cook without turning for 20 minutes.
3. Place bundle on serving plate and open foil. Serve in foil.

SERVES 6.

Nantucket Barbecued Bass

A tangy fish barbecue that pays off in large flavor despite its easy preparation.

BARBECUE

PREPARATION TIME: 30 MINUTES

2 pounds striped bass steaks
½ cup oil
½ cup sesame seeds
⅓ cup cognac

⅓ cup lemon juice
3 tablespoons soy sauce
1 teaspoon salt
1 large clove garlic, crushed

1. Place a single layer of serving-sized bass steaks in a shallow baking dish. Combine remaining ingredients, pour over fish, and let stand for 30 minutes, turning once. Remove fish, but save sauce for basting.
2. Place fish in well-greased hinged wire grills. Place on grill about 4 inches from moderately hot coals. Cook for 8 minutes.
3. Baste with sauce, turn, and cook for 7 to 10 minutes or until fish flakes easily with a fork.

SERVES 6.

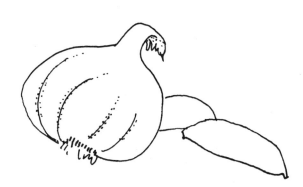

New England Fish Chowder

Float some crumbled pilot crackers on top of the finished chowder to increase the attractiveness of this robust meal.

TOP BURNER   PREPARATION TIME: 30 MINUTES

2 pounds fresh cod or pollock fillets   4 cups boiling water
¼ pound salt pork   4 cups milk
3 large onions, sliced   Salt and pepper to taste
4 cups diced potatoes

1. Cut fish fillets into 2-inch pieces. Dice the salt pork and fry slowly in a heavy pot until crisp and golden. Remove and save pork.
2. Fry onions in pork fat until translucent. Add potatoes and boiling water. Cook until potatoes are almost tender. Then add fish and cook until fish flakes easily with a fork (about 15 minutes).
3. Add milk. Season to taste with salt and pepper. Bring to serving temperature over low heat, being careful not to boil. Garnish with cooked, diced salt pork and crackers.

SERVES 6.

Quick Barbecued Fish Steaks

The sauce adds a zesty touch to this barbecuing delight.

BARBECUE OR OVEN

PREPARATION TIME: 30 MINUTES

2 tablespoons butter
¼ cup catsup
3 tablespoons Worcestershire sauce

½ teaspoon salt
2 pounds halibut steak or other
   firm-fleshed fish

1. Melt butter in a small saucepan and stir in catsup, Worcestershire sauce, and salt.
2. Place fish on grill over hot coals (or in broiler pan under broiler) and brush generously with sauce. Grill, turning once and brushing with sauce, until fish flakes easily with fork.

SERVES 4.

Pan-Fried Mackerel

When preparing seafood, simplicity is often best—and tastiest.

TOP BURNER   PREPARATION TIME: 20 MINUTES

4 mackerel fillets   Salt and pepper to taste
1 cup milk   1 tablespoon parsley flakes
Flour   Lemon wedges
6 tablespoons butter

1. Wash mackerel in cold water and pat dry. Dip each fillet in milk and roll in flour until coated.
2. Melt 3 tablespoons butter in a skillet, but do not burn. Add fish and brown on one side. Turn carefully and brown other side.
3. Remove from skillet. Salt and pepper to taste and sprinkle with parsley. Melt additional butter in pan and pour over fish. Serve with lemon wedges.

SERVES 4.

Tuna Pilaf

Give your dinner a touch of Middle Eastern elegance—without fuss and bother.

TOP BURNER   PREPARATION TIME: 25 MINUTES

2 cans tuna   3 cups cooked rice
1 small onion, sliced   3 tablespoons soy sauce
½ cup diced celery
1 10-ounce package frozen mixed vegetables, thawed

1. Drain oil from canned tuna. Place tuna in large saucepan. Add onion, celery, and mixed vegetables. Cook until vegetables are tender but not brown.
2. Add rice and soy sauce. Stir gently, cooking slowly until thoroughly mixed and heated.

SERVES 6.

Practical Fish Guide

SPECIES OF FISH	FAT OR LEAN	BROIL	BAKE	BOIL STEAM POACH	FRY SAUTÉ
Alewife	Fat		Best	Good	
Barracuda	Fat	Good	Best		Fair
Black bass	Lean	Good	Good		Good
Bloater	Fat				Best
Bluefish	Fat	Good	Best		Fair
Bonito	Fat	Good	Best		Fair
Buffalo fish	Lean	Good	Best		Fair
Bullhead	Lean		Fair	Good	Best
Butterfish	Fat	Good	Fair		Best
Carp	Lean	Good	Best		Fair
Catfish	Lean			Good	Best
Cod	Lean	Best	Good	Fair	
Croaker (Hardhead)	Lean	Good	Fair		Best
Drum (Redfish)	Lean		Best	Good	
Eel	Fat		Good	Fair	Best
Flounder	Lean	Good	Fair		Best
Fluke	Lean	Good	Fair		Best
Grouper	Lean		Best		
Haddock	Lean	Best	Good	Fair	
Hake	Lean	Fair	Best	Good	
Halibut	Fat	Best	Good	Fair	
Herring, Lake	Lean	Good	Fair		Best
Herring, Sea	Fat	Best	Fair		Good
Hog snapper (Grunt)	Lean	Good			Best
Jewfish	Lean		Best		
Kingfish	Lean	Best	Good	Fair	
King mackerel	Fat	Best	Good		
Lake trout	Fat	Fair	Best		Good
Ling cod	Lean	Best	Good	Fair	
Mackerel	Fat	Best	Good	Fair	
Mango snapper	Lean	Good			Best
Mullet	Fat	Best	Good		Fair
Muskellunge	Lean	Best	Good		Fair
Perch	Lean	Good	Fair		Best
Pickerel	Lean	Fair	Good		Best
Pike	Lean	Fair	Good		Best
Pollock	Lean	Fair	Good	Best	
Pompano	Fat	Best	Good		Fair
Porgies (Scup)	Fat	Good	Fair		Best
Redfish (Channel bass)	Lean	Good	Best		
Red snapper	Lean	Good	Best	Good	
Robalo (Snook)	Lean	Good	Best		
Rockfish	Lean		Good	Best	
Rosefish	Lean		Good		Best
Sablefish (Black cod)	Fat			Good	
Salmon	Fat	Good	Best	Fair	

SPECIES OF FISH	FAT OR LEAN	BROIL	BAKE	BOIL STEAM POACH	FRY SAUTÉ
Sardine	Fat		Best		
Sea bass	Fat	Best	Fair		Good
Sea trout	Fat	Best	Good		Fair
Shad	Fat	Good	Best		Fair
Shark (Grayfish)	Fat		Best	Good	
Sheepshead, freshwater	Lean		Good	Best	
Sheepshead, saltwater	Lean	Best	Good		Fair
Smelt	Lean	Good	Fair		Best
Snapper	Lean	Good	Best	Fair	
Sole	Lean	Good	Fair		Best
Spanish mackerel	Fat	Best	Good		Fair
Spot	Lean				
Striped bass (Rockfish)	Fat		Good	Best	
Sturgeon	Fat	Good	Best	Fair	
Suckers	Lean	Good	Fair		Best
Sunfish (Pumpkinseed)	Lean	Good			Best
Swordfish	Fat	Best	Good	Fair	
Tautog (Blackfish)	Lean	Best	Good		Fair
Trout	Lean	Good	Fair		Best
Tuna	Fat	Fair	Best	Good	
Walleye (Pike perch)	Lean			Best	
Weakfish (Sea trout)	Lean	Best	Good		Fair
Whitefish	Fat	Good	Best		Fair
Whiting (Silver hake)	Lean			Best	
Yellowtail	Fat		Good	Best	

Timetable for Cooking Fish

METHOD OF COOKING	MARKET FORM	AMOUNT FOR 6 SERVINGS	COOKING TEMPERATURE	APPROXIMATE COOKING TIME
Baking	Dressed	3 pounds	350° F.	40 to 60 minutes
	Pan-dressed	3 pounds	350° F.	25 to 30 minutes
	Fillets or steaks	2 pounds	350° F.	20 to 25 minutes
	Frozen fried fish portions	12 portions (2½ to 3 ounces each)	400° F.	15 to 20 minutes
	Frozen fried fish sticks	24 sticks (¾ to 1¼ ounces each)	400° F.	15 to 20 minutes

METHOD OF COOKING	MARKET FORM	AMOUNT FOR 6 SERVINGS	COOKING TEMPERATURE	APPROXIMATE COOKING TIME
Broiling	Pan-dressed	3 pounds		10 to 16 minutes (turning once)
	Fillets or steaks	2 pounds		10 to 15 minutes
	Frozen fried fish portions	12 portions (2½ to 3 ounces each)		10 to 15 minutes
	Frozen fried fish sticks	24 sticks (¾ to 1¼ ounces each)		10 to 15 minutes
Charcoal broiling	Pan-dressed	3 pounds	Moderate	10 to 16 minutes (turning once)
	Fillets or steaks	2 pounds	Moderate	10 to 16 minutes (turning once)
	Frozen fried fish portions	12 portions (2½ to 3 ounces each)	Moderate	8 to 10 minutes (turning once)
	Frozen fried fish sticks	24 sticks (¾ to 1¼ ounces each)	Moderate	8 to 10 minutes (turning once)
Deep-fat frying	Pan-dressed	3 pounds	350° F.	3 to 5 minutes
	Fillets or steaks	2 pounds	350° F.	3 to 5 minutes
	Frozen raw breaded fish portions	12 portions (2½ to 3 ounces each)	350° F.	3 to 5 minutes
Oven frying	Pan-dressed	3 pounds	500° F.	15 to 20 minutes
	Fillets or steaks	2 pounds	500° F.	10 to 15 minutes
Pan frying	Pan-dressed	3 pounds	Moderate	8 to 10 minutes (turning once)
	Fillets or steaks	2 pounds	Moderate	8 to 10 minutes (turning once)
	Frozen raw breaded or frozen fried fish portions	12 portions (2½ to 3 ounces each)	Moderate	8 to 10 minutes
	Frozen fried fish sticks	24 sticks (¾ to 1¼ ounces each)	Moderate	8 to 10 minutes (turning once)
Poaching	Fillets or steaks	2 pounds	Simmer	5 to 10 minutes
Steaming	Fillets or steaks	1½ pounds	Boil	5 to 10 minutes

Meats

Beef Fondue

You won't want to stop eating just because your fondue fork becomes very hot. Slip the cooked beef onto your plate and use a dinner fork for eating.

TOP BURNER   PREPARATION TIME: 15 MINUTES

3 cups cooking oil
½ cup water
1 envelope onion soup mix
1½ pounds trimmed beef tenderloin,
  cubed

1. Combine oil, water, and soup mix in a medium saucepan and bring to boil.
2. Remove to fondue pot or heated casserole.
3. Spear beef cubes with long-handled forks and hold each beef cube in boiling mixture until cooked to desired doneness. Serve with individual bowls of dipping sauces such as mustard relish, horseradish in sour cream, or chutney sauce.

SERVES 6.

Beef Kabobs

Remember to marinate the beef during the afternoon for an evening's barbecue that everyone will remember.

BARBECUE

PREPARATION TIME: 20 MINUTES

1 envelope onion soup mix
1 cup dry red wine
¼ cup cooking oil
1 tablespoon soy sauce
1 clove garlic, crushed
½ teaspoon pepper

2 pounds boneless beef, cut into strips or cubed
12 mushroom caps
3 medium quartered tomatoes
2 small green peppers, chunked

1. In a baking pan, combine the soup mix, wine, oil, soy sauce, garlic, and pepper to make marinade. Add the meat, coating thoroughly, and marinate 4 to 5 hours. Save marinade for basting.
2. Alternately thread the meat, mushrooms, tomatoes, and green peppers on skewers. Place over hot coals and grill quickly. Turn once and baste with marinade.

SERVES 6.

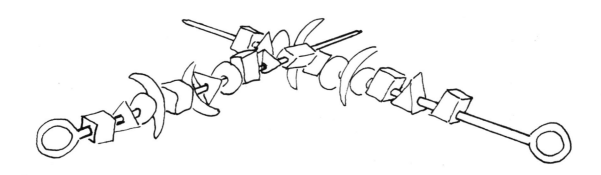

Beef Stroganoff

Served over a bed of rice, this steak in creamy mushroom sauce will bring everyone back for seconds.

PREPARATION TIME: 40 MINUTES

⅓ cup flour
1 teaspoon salt
¼ teaspoon garlic powder
¼ teaspoon pepper
1 pound sirloin tip steak, cut in very thin strips
½ cup finely chopped onion
¼ cup fat or oil

1 10-ounce can condensed cream of mushroom soup
1 8-ounce can sliced mushrooms, drained
1 cup sour cream
Cooked rice
Paprika
Parsley

1. Combine flour, salt, garlic powder, and pepper. Coat meat strips thoroughly with flour mixture.
2. Heat oil in a large skillet. Add meat and brown on all sides. Add onion and cook until onion is tender. Drain excess oil.
3. Add soup and mushrooms. Cover and simmer for 10 to 15 minutes. Blend in sour cream and remove from heat.
4. Serve over rice, sprinkled with paprika and garnished with parsley.

SERVES 6.

Beef-Tomato Stew

A minimum of fuss is involved in preparing this robust stew.

TOP BURNER   PREPARATION TIME: 35 MINUTES

2 large onions, chopped
1 clove garlic, minced
2 tablespoons vegetable oil
½ pound ground beef
4 cups canned tomatoes

½ cup uncooked rice
1 cup water
Salt to taste
Pepper to taste

1. Place onions, garlic, oil, and ground beef in deep saucepan. Cook until meat is browned and onions are tender.
2. Add tomatoes, rice, water, salt, and pepper. Cover and cook over low heat about 25 minutes, or until rice is tender.

SERVES 6.

Chinese Beef and Greens

Primarily a vegetable dish to be served over rice. Chicken may be substituted for beef in this quick, savory meal.

TOP BURNER   PREPARATION TIME: 25 MINUTES

1 small bunch bok choy (or Chinese cabbage, spinach, other greens)
1 onion, chopped
1 tablespoon oil

⅓ cup thinly sliced or ground beef
2 tablespoons soy sauce
2 teaspoons cornstarch
½ cup water

1. Separate greens from stems and cut stems in 1-inch pieces.
2. Heat oil in a skillet and fry onion for 2 minutes. Add the meat and cook until the bright red is gone. Add stems of vegetables and cook, stirring constantly, for about 2 minutes.
3. Mix together soy sauce, cornstarch, and water, and add to skillet. Add the leaves of the greens. Cover and cook until the leaves are just limp. Serve over rice.

SERVES 4.

French Beef Stew

This tasty, hearty stew can be prepared ahead of time to satisfy those robust outdoor appetites.

TOP BURNER

PREPARATION TIME: 2 HOURS

2 tablespoons shortening or cooking oil
2 4-ounce cans sliced mushrooms, drained
2 cloves garlic, minced
2½ pounds chuck beef, cubed
1½ tablespoons flour

1 envelope onion soup mix
¼ teaspoon dried thyme
2 bay leaves
1 cup red wine
1½ cups water

1. Heat oil or shortening in a heavy saucepan and cook mushrooms and garlic until golden. Add cubed beef and brown well.
2. Stir in flour, soup mix, thyme, bay leaves, wine, and water. Bring to a boil, stirring occasionally.
3. Reduce heat, cover, and simmer 1½ to 2 hours or until meat is tender.

SERVES 6.

Grilled London Broil

Here's an easy way to turn a plain barbecued steak into a savory London Broil.

BARBECUE

PREPARATION TIME: 30 MINUTES

3 tablespoons salad oil
2 tablespoons chopped fresh parsley
1 tablespoon lemon juice
2 tablespoons salt
¾ teaspoon crushed rosemary

½ teaspoon pepper
2 cloves garlic, crushed
Unseasoned meat tenderizer
1 2-pound, top-round beef steak, about 2
    inches thick

1. Combine salad oil, parsley, lemon juice, salt, rosemary, pepper, and garlic cloves and mix well. Set aside.
2. Sprinkle meat tenderizer on steak according to label directions and place steak on grill about 5 inches above medium hot coals. Brushing frequently with oil mixture, grill about 15 minutes (or to desired doneness) on each side, turning once. Slice meat diagonally across grain into thin slices before serving.

SERVES 6.

Hamburger Stroganoff

Tired of the same old hamburger? Try this easy recipe to give a familiar dish new zest.

TOP BURNER   PREPARATION TIME: 30 MINUTES

½ pound lean ground beef
1 tablespoon butter
1 4-ounce can sliced mushrooms, drained
2 tablespoons chopped onion
2 tablespoons flour
1½ cups beef broth
½ teaspoon salt

Dash pepper
1 tablespoon catsup
½ cup sour cream
8 ounces rigatoni
Minced parsley

1. Melt butter in skillet, add ground beef and lightly brown, stirring frequently. Add mushrooms and onions and cook about 3 minutes. Remove from heat and blend in flour.
2. Add the beef broth, salt, pepper, and catsup. Cook over low heat for 10 minutes, stirring occasionally. Blend in sour cream and heat for one more minute.
3. Meanwhile, boil macaroni for 12 to 14 minutes, or to desired tenderness, and then drain.
4. Serve stroganoff over macaroni, sprinkled with parsley.

SERVES 4.

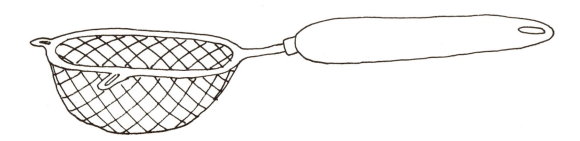

Hamburger Surprise

Layering vegetables and cheese over the meat turns plain hamburger into a novel meal.

TOP BURNER

PREPARATION TIME: 45 MINUTES

1 pound ground beef
Salt and pepper to taste
8 slices American cheese
½ cup chopped green pepper
½ cup chopped celery

¼ cup chopped onion
2 cups uncooked noodles
4 cups cooked or canned tomatoes
¼ cup water
1 green pepper, sliced in rings (optional)

1. Cook meat in skillet over moderate heat until lightly browned. Salt and pepper to taste.
2. Add remaining ingredients in layers as listed above. Raise heat and quickly bring to boil. Lower heat and cook for about 30 minutes until vegetables and noodles are tender.

SERVES 6.

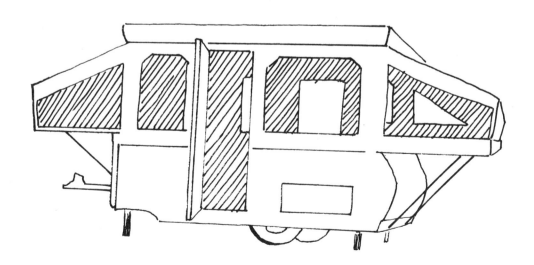

Harbor Stew

You don't have to be near water to enjoy this rich, savory stew.

TOP BURNER

PREPARATION TIME: 1 HOUR 30 MINUTES

2 tablespoons salad oil
2 pounds beef stew meat, cut in 1½-inch
  chunks
2 medium onions, quartered
1 teaspoon salt
6 whole allspice
1 bay leaf
⅛ teaspoon pepper

1 beef bouillon cube
Water
3 carrots, cut in thin strips
1 pound zucchini, thinly sliced
1 cup dried apricots
½ teaspoon sugar
1 tablespoon all-purpose flour

1. Heat oil in a Dutch oven or large saucepan. Add stew beef and brown well on all sides.
2. Add onions, seasonings, bouillon cube, and 2½ cups water. Bring to boil.
3. Reduce heat, cover, and simmer for 1 hour or until meat is tender. Add carrots to beef and cook 5 minutes.
4. Add zucchini, apricots, and sugar. Continue cooking 10 minutes more or until vegetables are tender. Remove and discard bay leaf.
5. Blend flour and ¼ cup water until smooth. Gradually stir into stew liquid.
6. Cook, stirring constantly, until sauce thickens and boils for 1 minute. Salt and pepper to taste and serve.

SERVES 6.

Honey Steak

The delicious marinade will give a smooth, new taste to any steak. It makes a cold steak sandwich the next day even more tasty.

BROILER OR BARBECUE   PREPARATION TIME: 20 MINUTES

Flank steak (about 1½ pounds)
½ cup soy sauce
½ cup honey

1. Mix soy sauce and honey together. Marinate steak in mixture for 1 hour, turning once.
2. Place in broiler or on grill about 3 inches above hot coals and cook to desired doneness. Save marinade to heat and serve with meat.
3. Cut steak on the diagonal into thin strips. Serve at once with remaining marinade.

SERVES 4 TO 6.

Liver and Onions

TOP BURNER   PREPARATION TIME: 40 MINUTES

1½ pounds beef liver, sliced   **¼ teaspoon pepper**
½ cup flour   **1 large onion, sliced**
2 tablespoons oil   **¼ cup water**
1½ teaspoons salt

1. Remove any skin from liver and coat liver with flour. In a large skillet, heat oil over moderate heat. Add liver and brown on one side.
2. Turn liver, sprinkle with seasonings, and cover with onions. Add water, cover pan tightly, and cook over low heat for 20 to 30 minutes, or until liver is tender.

SERVES 4.

Quick Goulash

Here's a quick, one-pan dish the whole family will relish.

TOP BURNER

PREPARATION TIME: 30 MINUTES

3 pats butter
1 pound ground beef
1 envelope onion soup mix
1 8-ounce can tomato sauce

24 ounces water (three sauce cans)
¼ pound elbow macaroni
Minced parsley

1. Melt butter in large skillet. Add beef and brown, stirring to separate particles.
2. Add onion soup mix, tomato sauce, and water. Bring to a boil. Add macaroni slowly and simmer for 15 minutes or until macaroni is tender. Stir frequently, and add more water if necessary. Garnish with parsley before serving.

SERVES 4.

Steak au Poivre

The classic steak, a perennial favorite for its simplicity and unsurpassed flavor.

TOP BURNER

PREPARATION TIME: 35 MINUTES

1 to 2 tablespoons coarsely ground black pepper
1 4-pound boned sirloin steak, 2 inches thick

1 teaspoon salt
½ cup dry red wine

1. Rub pepper into both sides of steak. Let stand at room temperature for ½ hour.
2. Lightly grease a large heavy skillet. Heat until hot. Sprinkle both sides of steak with salt. Cook in skillet for 8 to 10 minutes on each side or until done as desired.
3. Remove meat to serving platter. Add wine to juices in pan. Cook, stirring, for 1 minute. Pour over steak. Slice and serve.

SERVES 6 TO 8.

Stuffed Peppers

With these peppers, the secret is in the stuffing.

TOP BURNER   PREPARATION TIME: 75 MINUTES

1 slightly beaten egg
½ cup milk
⅔ cup soft bread cubes
1 teaspoon salt
⅛ teaspoon pepper
¼ teaspoon celery salt
⅛ teaspoon sage
2 tablespoons seedless raisins
1 pound lean ground beef

¼ cup chopped onion
2 tablespoons olive oil
4 medium green peppers, topped
  and seeded
3 8-ounce cans tomato sauce
½ teaspoon garlic salt
½ teaspoon oregano leaves
½ teaspoon basil leaves

1. In a large bowl, mix together egg, milk, bread cubes, salt, pepper, celery salt, sage, and raisins, and let stand 5 minutes. Add the beef and mix thoroughly.
2. Heat oil in a large pan, add onion, and sauté until tender. Remove from heat. Combine half of onion with meat mixture. Stuff peppers with mixture.
3. Add the tomato sauce, garlic salt, oregano, and basil to the remaining onion in pan and stir. Place the stuffed peppers upright in the sauce.
4. Cover and simmer about 45 minutes or until peppers are tender. Uncover and cook another 5 to 10 minutes, occasionally basting with sauce.

SERVES 4.

Veal and Peppers

For those special occasions, this one-pan meal will draw raves for the cook.

TOP BURNER

PREPARATION TIME: 45 MINUTES

4 large green peppers, cut into ½-inch strips
1½ pounds thinly sliced veal cutlets, cut into 2-inch strips
½ teaspoon salt

2 tablespoons butter
2 beef bouillon cubes dissolved in 1½ cups water
1 large tomato, peeled and cut into eighths
1 6-ounce can mushrooms, drained

1. Parboil peppers in salted water for 3 minutes and drain.
2. Sprinkle veal with salt. Melt butter in a large skillet and brown veal quickly. Stir in bouillon and mushrooms, blending well.
3. Add peppers and tomato, cover, and simmer 20 minutes or until veal is tender.

SERVES 6.

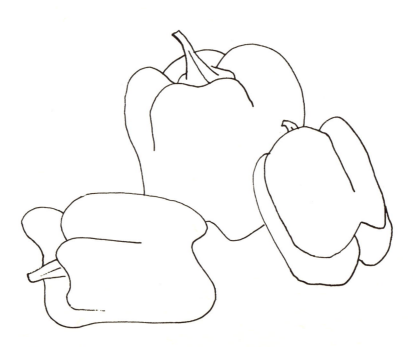

Lamb Curry

1½ pounds boneless stew lamb, cut in
  1-inch cubes
½ cup finely chopped onion
1½ teaspoons salt
⅛ teaspoon pepper
2 teaspoons curry powder
½ teaspoon ginger
1 teaspoon sugar

2 cups water
1 cup chopped tart apple
¼ cup raisins
2 tablespoons cornstarch
¼ cup water
3 cups cooked rice
⅓ cup chutney

1. In a heavy saucepan, brown meat and then add onion, seasonings, sugar, and 2 cups water. Cover and simmer 1 hour or until meat is tender.
2. Add apple and raisins and cook 15 minutes more.
3. In a bowl, mix cornstarch with ¼ cup water. Stir into lamb mixture. Stirring constantly, cook until thickened. Serve over hot cooked rice, garnished with chutney if desired.

SERVES 6.

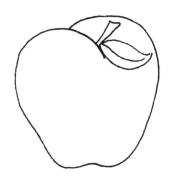

Lamb Stew

The aroma of this bubbling stew will bring everyone to the dinner table on time.

TOP BURNER

PREPARATION TIME: 2 HOURS

2 tablespoons butter
2 onions, chopped
4 carrots, chopped
2 turnips, diced
3 pounds lamb, cubed
5 cups beef broth
5 cups water

2 pounds peeled and diced potatoes
1 leek, diced
¼ teaspoon rosemary
¼ teaspoon dill seed
Salt to taste
Pepper to taste

1. Melt butter in a large saucepan or Dutch oven and sauté onions, carrots, and turnips, stirring constantly, until onion is transparent.
2. Remove vegetables and add lamb. Sauté lamb, stirring, until browned on all sides.
3. Put vegetables back into pan and add broth, water, potatoes, leek, and all seasonings, and simmer uncovered for about 2 hours.

SERVES 4 TO 6.

Asparagus Rolled in Ham

Try this shortcut to a tempting French meal complete in one dish.

OVEN

PREPARATION TIME: 1 HOUR

1 1-pound can white asparagus
12 thin slices boiled or baked ham
¼ cup Dijon mustard
1 cup sour cream
2 cups grated Bonbel, Port Salut, or
   St. Paulin cheese
6 cups diced cooked potatoes

½ cup sliced celery
¼ cup sliced dill pickle
2 tablespoons finely chopped scallions
⅓ cup olive oil
¼ cup tarragon vinegar
2 teaspoons Dijon mustard
½ teaspoon salt

1. Open bottom end of asparagus can, drain liquid, and slide asparagus spears onto flat plate.
2. Spread ham slices with the ¼ cup of mustard. Place an asparagus spear at one end of each ham slice and roll up. Place the rolled ham slices in a shallow oblong casserole pan.
3. Blend the sour cream and cheese and spoon over ham rolls.
4. Combine remaining ingredients in a separate bowl and toss well. Place the mixture in the casserole with the ham rolls.
5. Cover and bake in a preheated oven at 350° for 30 to 35 minutes or until hot.

SERVES 6.

Barbecued Frankfurters

Here's a way to give a new twist to frankfurters, an old camping standby.

TOP BURNER   PREPARATION TIME: 30 MINUTES

¾ cup catsup   1 tablespoon prepared mustard
¾ cup water   2 teaspoons Worcestershire sauce
¼ cup chopped onion   1 clove garlic, mashed
2 tablespoons brown sugar   1 pound frankfurters (cut in one-inch slices)
2 tablespoons lemon juice

1. In a saucepan combine catsup, water, onion, brown sugar, lemon juice, mustard, Worcestershire, and garlic. Cover and simmer for 10 minutes.
2. Add frankfurters, cover, and simmer another 10 minutes, stirring occasionally.

SERVES 4.

Barbecued Pork Chops

Pork chops can be a barbecuing treat, particularly when cooked with this special sauce.

BARBECUE   PREPARATION TIME: 45 MINUTES

½ teaspoon rosemary   ¼ teaspoon thyme
1 tablespoon soy sauce   ¼ teaspoon sage
2 teaspoons oil   ¼ teaspoon garlic powder
½ teaspoon seasoned salt   6 ¾-inch pork chops

1. Crush rosemary and mix well with all other ingredients except pork chops. Brush mixture on both sides of chops.
2. Place chops on grill about 6 inches from hot coals. Sear both sides. Raise grill and cook slowly for 35 minutes, brushing occasionally with sauce mixture.

SERVES 6.

Hearty Ribs and Chicken

Plan ahead to let the ribs and chicken marinate, and you'll have a barbecued feast that could become your favorite.

BARBECUE

PREPARATION TIME: 1 HOUR 30 MINUTES

5 pounds pork spareribs, trimmed of excess
   fat
2 3-pound broiler-fryer chickens, quartered
Salt and pepper to taste
2 cups catsup
2 cups pineapple juice

2 cups dry red wine
1 tablespoon salt
½ cup Worcestershire sauce
1 teaspoon Tabasco sauce (optional)
1 onion, grated
2 cloves garlic, mashed

1. Sprinkle ribs and chicken with salt and pepper on all sides and place in a large pan.
2. Combine all remaining ingredients, mixing thoroughly, and pour over ribs and chicken.
3. Let marinate for 2 hours at room temperature, or marinate in refrigerator overnight, turning at least once.
4. Drain ribs and chicken thoroughly. Place on grill 8 inches above moderately hot coals and barbecue for 1 hour or until done.
5. Pour marinade into a saucepan and heat on grill. Turn ribs and chicken every 15 minutes and brush frequently with marinade.
6. Cut cooked ribs into individual pieces. Serve marinade as dipping sauce for ribs and chicken.

SERVES 8.

Jambalaya

Serve this hearty jambalaya with toasted bread poles for a unique grilled meal.

BARBECUE   PREPARATION TIME: 1 HOUR

1 cup butter   1 cup converted rice
1 large onion, chopped   2 1-pound cans stewed tomatoes
1 clove garlic, chopped   1 cup water
1 green pepper, chopped   1 10-ounce package frozen peas
1 smoked ham steak, 1 to 1½ pounds, cut   Salt
   into 1-inch cubes   Pepper

1. In large skillet about 8 inches above medium-hot coals, melt butter and sauté onion, garlic, and green pepper until wilted (about 5 minutes).
2. Add ham and rice. Cook and stir for 10 minutes. Stir in tomatoes and water. Cover tightly and simmer for 20 to 25 minutes or until rice is tender and liquid is absorbed. Stir occasionally during cooking to prevent sticking.
3. Add peas and season to taste with salt and pepper. Cook until peas are heated through.

SERVES 6.

Toasted Bread Poles

Crispy barbecued bread goes perfectly with grilled jambalaya.

BARBECUE   PREPARATION TIME: 15 MINUTES

1 unsliced loaf of bread
½ cup butter
2 tablespoons minced chives

1. Cut loaf of bread into halves lengthwise and cut each half into 3 pieces.
2. Melt butter in pan and stir in chives. Roll pieces of bread in butter mixture or use a brush to cover bread with butter.
3. Place bread on grill over medium-hot coals and cook about 3 to 4 minutes on each side. Turn bread poles on all 4 sides until all pieces are brown and crusty.

SERVES 6.

Apple Brandy Pork Chops

This rich dinner, simmered in a sauce of apple brandy, orange juice, and cream, is a favorite in Normandy.

TOP BURNER

PREPARATION TIME: 1 HOUR 25 MINUTES

6 1-inch thick center cut pork chops
Salt and pepper to taste
½ cup apple brandy
1 clove garlic, chopped
1 6-ounce can frozen orange juice
  concentrate (undiluted)

2 tablespoons Dijon mustard
½ pint heavy cream
1 tablespoon cornstarch
1 6-ounce can whole mushrooms, drained

1. Sprinkle chops with salt and pepper. Place in a large skillet and brown on both sides over high heat. Pour in the apple brandy and set aflame.
2. Add the garlic, orange juice concentrate, and mustard. Cover and simmer about 1 hour or until the chops are tender.
3. Remove the chops to a platter and keep warm.
4. In a bowl, mix the heavy cream and cornstarch. Stir into the pan juices. Cook over low heat, stirring constantly, until the sauce bubbles and thickens. Add the mushrooms and reheat.
5. Place the chops back into the sauce and reheat until bubbly.

SERVES 6.

Chinese-Style Pork Chops

Plain old pork chops will never be the same once you try this recipe.

TOP BURNER   PREPARATION TIME: 1 HOUR

6 pork chops
2 tablespoons oil
1 8-ounce bottle sweet and sour sauce
1 14-ounce can pineapple chunks

2 green peppers, cut into strips
¼ cup sliced water chestnuts
2 medium tomatoes, cut into wedges
2 tablespoons flour

1. Heat oil in a large, heavy skillet and brown chops. Add sweet and sour sauce, cover, and simmer until meat is tender.
2. Drain pineapple chunks, saving ½ cup syrup. Add pineapple, green peppers, and water chestnuts to chops. Cover and simmer until vegetables are crisp and tender. Add tomatoes and heat.
3. Arrange meat, fruit, and vegetables on serving platter.
4. Gradually add pineapple syrup to flour and mix until smooth. Add to sauce and stir until thickened. Serve with meat.

SERVES 6.

Pork Fried Rice

A Chinese specialty the whole family will love.

TOP BURNER   PREPARATION TIME: 25 MINUTES

½ cup diced scallions
2 tablespoons vegetable oil
1 clove garlic, minced
1 cup chopped cooked pork

4 cups cooked rice
2 tablespoons soy sauce
1 egg

1. Heat oil in large frying pan. Add scallions, garlic, and meat. Cook, stirring, over medium heat until onion is tender.
2. Add rice and soy sauce. Lower heat and cook 10 minutes.
3. Beat egg well and stir into rice mixture. Cook over low heat, stirring constantly, for 5 minutes.

SERVES 6.

Rocky Mountain Scramble

This quick and easy dish will add zing to your morning and satisfy those early morning appetites after a good night's sleep in camp.

TOP BURNER

PREPARATION TIME: 15 MINUTES

6 slices of bacon
1 tablespoon butter
1 cup canned or defrosted corn kernels, thoroughly drained
½ cup finely chopped green pepper

¼ cup finely chopped pimiento
1 teaspoon salt
⅛ teaspoon freshly ground black pepper
6 eggs

1. Fry bacon over moderate heat in a large, ungreased skillet until crisp. Transfer slices to paper towel to drain.
2. Pour off all but about 3 tablespoons of the bacon fat, and add butter to skillet. Stir in corn over moderate heat for 1 to 2 minutes. Add pimiento, green pepper, salt, and black pepper. Stirring frequently, cook uncovered for 5 minutes or until vegetables are tender.
3. Pour lightly beaten eggs into skillet mixture and stir constantly. Cook over low heat until eggs are creamy. Do not overcook or eggs will become dry. Place egg mixture on serving plate and top with bacon slices.

SERVES 4.

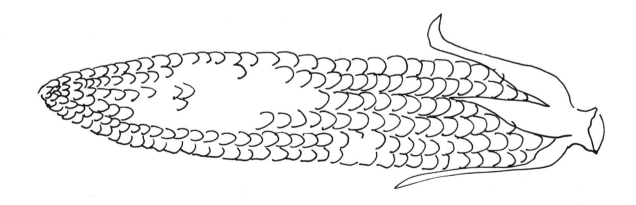

Sweet and Sour Pork

This Chinese-inspired recipe will prove deliciously that opposites attract.

TOP BURNER

PREPARATION TIME: 1 HOUR 15 MINUTES

1½ pounds boneless pork, cubed
Flour
Salt and pepper
2 tablespoons oil
½ cup barbecue sauce

¼ cup vinegar
¼ cup water
1 green pepper, cut into strips
1 10-ounce jar pineapple preserves

1. Combine salt, pepper, and flour. Coat meat well on both sides. Heat oil in large skillet and brown pork.
2. Add barbecue sauce, vinegar, and water. Cover and simmer for 1 hour, adding green pepper and preserves during last 15 minutes. (May be served with cooked white rice, if desired.)

SERVES 6.

Tangy Spareribs

The spicy basting sauce turns barbecued spareribs into a memorable meal.

BARBECUE   PREPARATION TIME: 1 HOUR

5 pounds lean spareribs   1 tablespoon seasoned salt
½ cup soy sauce   1 teaspoon dry mustard
½ cup dry sherry   1 teaspoon ginger
½ cup tomato catsup   1 teaspoon garlic powder
2 tablespoons minced onion   1 teaspoon lemon and pepper seasoning

1. Trim excess fat from spareribs. Combine all remaining ingredients and mix well.
2. Make a drip pan of heavy foil and place it under the grill. Arrange hot coals around drip pan. Place ribs on grill about 6 inches from coals. Cook for 30 minutes, turning ribs every 10 minutes.
3. Then brush both sides of ribs with basting sauce and cook another 30 minutes, or until ribs are well done, turning and brushing frequently.

SERVES 4.

Poultry

Baked Chicken with Mushroom Sauce

The rich and creamy mushroom sauce adds just the right touch to baked chicken.

OVEN

PREPARATION TIME: 1 HOUR

4 small, or 2 large split chicken breasts
1 envelope seasoned coating mix for chicken
1 10-ounce can condensed cream of mushroom soup

½ cup chicken broth (or ¼ cup water and ¼ cup dry sherry)

1. Following instructions on package, coat chicken with seasoned coating mix. Arrange in a single layer in an *ungreased* shallow baking pan. Bake at 400° for 20 minutes.
2. Combine soup and chicken broth (or water and sherry). Pour a little of the sauce over the chicken, leaving part of the browned chicken uncovered. Pour remaining sauce around the chicken in baking pan.
3. Bake about 20 minutes longer or until tender. Stir sauce in the pan and serve with the chicken.

SERVES 4.

Chicken à la King

Plan to serve chicken à la king as a "leftover" meal the night after a big chicken feast.

TOP BURNER

PREPARATION TIME: 20 MINUTES

1 cup frozen green peas
2 tablespoons finely chopped onion
¼ cup chopped green pepper
⅓ cup boiling water
⅔ cup flour
1 cup cold milk
2 cups chicken broth
2 teaspoons salt

Pepper to taste
½ teaspoon poultry seasoning
2 cups diced cooked chicken (or turkey)
1 4-ounce can mushroom stems and pieces, drained and chopped
1 tablespoon chopped pimiento
Cooked rice, toast, or biscuits

1. Bring ⅓ cup water to a boil and add peas, onion, and green pepper. Cook 5 minutes in a covered pan. Drain and save the liquid.
2. Blend flour with milk. Combine vegetable cooking liquid, broth, and seasonings. Slowly stir in flour mixture. Stirring constantly, bring to a boil and cook 1 minute.
3. Add the chicken, cooked vegetables, mushrooms and pimiento. Bring to serving temperature and serve on rice, toast, or biscuits.

SERVES 4.

Chicken and Sausage Mixed Grill

The sizzling drippings of the sausages onto the coals give the chicken a spicy, smoky flavor that everyone will enjoy.

BARBECUE

PREPARATION TIME: 1 HOUR

½ cup butter
1 medium clove garlic, crushed
¾ teaspoon salt
¾ teaspoon crushed summer savory
½ teaspoon paprika

⅛ teaspoon ground cinnamon
⅛ teaspoon crushed tarragon
1 3-pound broiler-fryer chicken, cut up
1 pound sweet Italian pork sausages

1. Melt the butter and stir in the garlic, salt, savory, paprika, cinnamon, and tarragon.
2. Place chicken and sausages on grill about 4 inches from medium hot coals and brush with butter mixture. Basting and turning sausage and chicken occasionally, grill about 30 to 40 minutes or until chicken is tender. Serve with Spanish Rice.

SERVES 6.

Chicken Casserole

This savory Italian dish will give your family a nutritious, one-pot meal that's sure to bring them back for seconds!

TOP BURNER

PREPARATION TIME: 45 MINUTES

3½ pound fryer chicken, cut up
2 tablespoons flour
2 teaspoons salt
½ teaspoon ground pepper
¼ cup olive oil
1 clove garlic, minced

½ cup dry white wine
1 cup peeled diced tomatoes
⅛ teaspoon rosemary
2 tablespoons minced parsley
¼ pound sliced mushrooms
2 tablespoons butter

1. Coat chicken thoroughly with mixture of flour, salt, and pepper. Heat oil in heavy, deep skillet and brown chicken.
2. Add garlic, wine, tomatoes, rosemary, and parsley to skillet. Cover skillet and cook over low heat for 20 minutes or until chicken is tender.
3. Sauté mushrooms in butter in a small saucepan while chicken is cooking. Add mushrooms to chicken just before serving.

SERVES 4 TO 6.

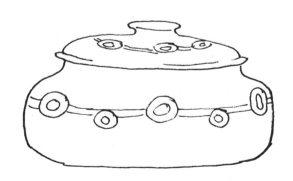

Chicken in Tangy Yogurt Sauce

A great way to use leftovers—it doesn't taste left-over.

TOP BURNER   PREPARATION TIME: 30 MINUTES

2 tablespoons butter
¼ pound sliced mushrooms (about 2 cups)
½ cup chopped onion
¼ cup chopped green pepper
1 cup mayonnaise
1 cup plain yogurt
½ teaspoon salt

Dash pepper
1½ cups chopped cooked chicken or
    turkey
1 cup cooked green peas
1 tablespoon chopped pimiento
Cooked rice

1. Melt butter in frying pan over medium heat. Add mushrooms, onion, and green pepper. Sauté, stirring frequently, about 5 minutes or until tender.
2. Mix together mayonnaise, yogurt, salt, and pepper. Add mixture to sautéed vegetables. Stir in chicken, peas, and pimiento.
3. Heat over low heat, stirring occasionally, for 10 to 15 minutes or until thoroughly heated. Serve with rice.

SERVES 4.

138

Chicken Kabob with Artichoke Hearts

As casual as a party—marinate ahead of time, then let each person cook his own to taste.

BARBECUE

PREPARATION TIME: 25 MINUTES PLUS MARINATING TIME

1 pint sour cream
1 tablespoon dill weed
Juice of 1 lemon
½ teaspoon salt
Black pepper to taste
Dash cayenne pepper

2 tablespoons instant minced onion
4 whole chicken breasts cut into 1- to
   1½-inch chunks
1 pound cherry tomatoes
2 cans artichoke hearts

1. Combine sour cream, dill, lemon juice, salt, pepper, cayenne, and instant minced onion with a wire whisk. Marinate chicken chunks in mixture for several hours or overnight.
2. Thread chicken on oiled skewers alternately with cherry tomatoes and artichoke hearts.
3. Grill over hot coals or under a broiler about 5 minutes on each side. (Be careful not to overcook or the chicken breasts will dry out.) Serve on a bed of rice.

SERVES 4.

Chicken Livers Hawaiian

If you can't get the children to eat chicken livers, try mixing them with pineapple chunks.

TOP BURNER

PREPARATION TIME: 30 MINUTES

1 pound chicken livers
¼ cup soy sauce
¼ cup vegetable oil
1 cup drained pineapple chunks
¼ cup toasted, slivered, blanched almonds
1¼ cups pineapple juice

2 tablespoons lemon juice
¼ teaspoon salt
¼ cup sugar
2 tablespoons cornstarch
2 cups cooked rice

1. Wash chicken livers under cold water and pat dry. Cut livers in half and dip the pieces in soy sauce. Heat the oil in a skillet and quickly brown the livers in it.
2. Add the pineapple and almonds, heat for less than a minute, and remove from heat.
3. In another pot, combine pineapple juice, lemon juice, salt, sugar, and cornstarch and stir over low heat until the sauce thickens and is clear and smooth.
4. Pour the sauce over chicken livers and serve on cooked rice.

SERVES 6.

Chicken Livers Italian

Fix a loaf of garlic bread and a tossed green salad, and you'll have a delicious, easy-to-prepare dinner.

TOP BURNER

PREPARATION TIME: 35 MINUTES

¾ pound chicken livers
3 tablespoons flour
⅛ teaspoon pepper
¾ teaspoon salt
1 tablespoon oil
18 small onions

½ pound fresh button mushrooms
4 cups diagonally sliced zucchini
¼ teaspoon thyme
½ teaspoon salt
1 tablespoon diced pimiento

1. Wash chicken livers under cold water and pat dry. Roll chicken livers in flour and season with salt and pepper.
2. Heat oil in skillet. Add chicken livers, and brown lightly over medium heat.
3. Add onions, mushrooms, zucchini, thyme, and ½ teaspoon salt. Cover and cook over medium heat for 15 to 25 minutes or until vegetables are tender.
4. Add pimiento and heat 1 minute longer.

SERVES 6.

Chicken Marengo

The perfect make-ahead dish—tastes even better the second day.

TOP BURNER   PREPARATION TIME: 1 HOUR 15 MINUTES

2 pounds chicken pieces
3 tablespoons olive oil
3 tablespoons butter
1 tablespoon chopped green onion
½ cup white wine
¼ cup soy sauce

1 tomato, peeled and chopped
½ cup chicken broth
¼ pound fresh mushrooms, sliced and
  sautéed in butter
Croutons

1. Sauté chicken in oil and butter in heavy skillet until well browned. Add green onions, wine, and soy sauce.
2. Cook, uncovered, over high heat until sauce is reduced by about half (about 10 minutes). Add tomato and chicken broth. Cover and simmer 45 minutes.
3. Transfer chicken to heated serving platter. Arrange mushrooms on chicken. Surround with croutons. Serve with sauce from the skillet on the side.

SERVES 4 TO 6.

Curried Chicken

Wondering what to do with that leftover chicken? Use this recipe to turn it into a savory meal.

TOP BURNER   PREPARATION TIME: 30 MINUTES

1 10-ounce can condensed cream of
  chicken soup
⅔ cup evaporated milk
¾ teaspoon curry powder
3 cups diced cooked chicken

1 cup drained canned pineapple chunks
½ cup sliced pimiento stuffed olives
2 cups cooked rice
Fresh sprigs parsley (optional)

1. Combine soup, milk, and curry powder in a medium-sized pot and heat slowly until well blended.
2. Add chicken, pineapple chunks, and olives. Heat to serving temperature.
3. Serve over cooked rice and garnish with sprigs of parsley, if desired.

SERVES 4 TO 6.

Fried Chicken with Cream Gravy

You can serve this chicken crisp, with the gravy in a sauce boat, or pour the gravy over the chicken before serving.

TOP BURNER AND OVEN   PREPARATION TIME: 50 MINUTES

3 to 4 cups vegetable oil
2½- to 3-pound chicken, cut into 8 serving
  pieces
2½ teaspoons salt

Pepper
½ cup plus 2 tablespoons flour
1 cup milk
1 cup heavy cream

1. Preheat oven to its lowest setting. Line a large shallow baking dish with a double thickness of paper towels and place the dish on the middle shelf of the oven.
2. Pour the vegetable oil into a large skillet or saucepan to a depth of 1 inch. Heat until it is very hot but not smoking.
3. Dry chicken with paper towels and season on all sides with 2 teaspoons of the salt and a pinch of pepper. Dip each piece of chicken in the ½ cup of flour, turn to coat it evenly, and shake off excess flour.
4. Fry the chicken legs and drumsticks, starting the pieces skin side down, and turning them frequently with tongs, until evenly browned (about 12 minutes). As they brown, drain the pieces of chicken in the paper-lined dish and keep them warm in the oven. Repeat until all pieces are fried.
5. Pour off all but a thin film of fat from the pan and add the 2 tablespoons of flour, mixing well. Pour in milk and cream slowly, stirring constantly, and cook over high heat until the gravy comes to a boil and thickens slightly. Reduce heat and simmer for 2 to 3 minutes. Add the remaining ½ teaspoon of salt and a dash of pepper.
6. Arrange the pieces of chicken on a platter. Pour gravy over it or serve gravy in a sauce boat on the side.

SERVES 4.

Lemony Cheese Chicken

Chicken takes on a subtle new flavor when prepared according to this simple recipe.

TOP BURNER

PREPARATION TIME: 20 MINUTES

4 boned chicken breasts
½ cup flour
½ cup grated Parmesan cheese
several sprigs fresh parsley, chopped (or 1
 teaspoon dry parsley flakes)

2 tablespoons butter
2 tablespoons oil
1 lemon
Salt and pepper

1. Mix flour, cheese, and parsley thoroughly in a plastic bag. Place chicken pieces in bag and shake until all pieces are lightly coated.
2. In a heavy skillet, melt butter and oil. Cook chicken 5 to 7 minutes on each side over medium heat. When turning chicken, sprinkle each side with salt and pepper and squeeze ½ lemon over the pieces.
3. Remove immediately to warm platter. Decorate with lemon wedges and parsley and pour juices from pan over the chicken. Serve at once.

SERVES 4.

Pineapple Chicken

This Chinese-inspired dish is a new twist for chicken.

TOP BURNER

PREPARATION TIME: 30 MINUTES

2 tablespoons soy sauce
½ teaspoon salt
¼ teaspoon pepper
½ teaspoon sugar
4 tablespoons salad oil
2 tablespoons cornstarch mixed with just
    enough cold water to make a paste

6 large chicken breasts, split lengthwise
1 12-ounce can pineapple chunks
2 cloves garlic, minced
Parsley for garnish

1. Mix soy sauce, salt, pepper, sugar, 1 tablespoon of the oil, and cornstarch paste in a bowl. Marinate chicken in the mixture for 3 minutes. Drain pineapple, reserving juice.
2. Heat the remaining oil in a skillet and sauté chicken until just underdone. Add the pineapple, cover, and cook for 5 minutes over medium heat.
3. Add the pineapple juice and garlic to the marinade in the bowl, and add this mixture to chicken.
4. Bring to a boil, stirring constantly until sauce thickens. Serve with parsley over rice.

SERVES 4 TO 6.

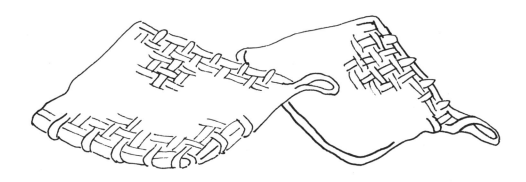

Southern Fried Chicken

You don't have to be from the South to prepare this perfect, crispy fried chicken.

TOP BURNER AND OVEN   PREPARATION TIME: 45 MINUTES

3 to 4 cups vegetable oil
2½- to 3-pound chicken, cut into 8 serving
　pieces
2 teaspoons salt

Pepper
1 egg, lightly beaten and combined with ½
　cup milk
1 cup flour

1. Preheat oven to its lowest setting. Line a large shallow baking dish with paper towels and place it in the center of the oven.
2. Pour vegetable oil into a large skillet or heavy saucepan to a depth of 1½ to 2 inches. Heat until it is very hot but not smoking.
3. Dry chicken with paper towels and season on all sides with salt and pepper. Dip the chicken pieces in the egg-and-milk mixture, then dip them in the flour, turning to coat lightly and evenly.
4. Fry chicken legs and drumsticks, starting them skin side down and turning frequently until evenly browned (about 12 minutes). As they brown, transfer them to the paper-lined dish and keep warm in the oven. Repeat until all pieces are fried.
5. When all pieces are fried, place on a serving platter and serve at once.

SERVES 4.

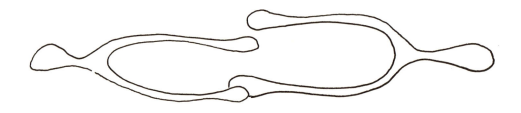

Turkey alla Genoa

A quick and easy version of an old Italian favorite.

TOP BURNER

PREPARATION TIME: 15 MINUTES

¼ cup milk
½ cup mayonnaise
½ cup finely shredded Cheddar or grated
   Parmesan cheese

Cooked turkey slices
1 10-ounce package frozen broccoli spears,
   cooked and drained
4 slices toast

1. Gradually stir milk into mayonnaise in saucepan. Heat over low heat until just hot. Stir in cheese until melted.
2. Arrange turkey and broccoli on toast. Spoon on cheese sauce.

SERVES 4.

Turkey Tetrazzini

TOP BURNER AND OVEN

PREPARATION TIME: 45 MINUTES

1 8-ounce package spaghetti
2 cups cutup cooked or canned turkey
¼ cup butter
½ cup sliced onions
¼ cup flour
¼ teaspoon pepper
1 teaspoon salt

½ teaspoon poultry seasoning
¼ teaspoon dry mustard
2 cups milk
1 cup shredded cheese
1 4-ounce can mushroom stems and pieces,
   with liquid

1. While preparing other ingredients, cook spaghetti according to directions on package. Drain.
2. In a medium-sized pot, sauté onion in butter until tender. Stir in flour and seasonings. Remove from heat.
3. Slowly stir in milk until mixture is smooth. Cook over medium heat until sauce is thickened. Add ½ cup cheese and stir until cheese melts. Add mushrooms.
4. Place a layer of spaghetti in a baking dish. Cover with a layer of turkey and add a layer of sauce. Repeat layers and finish with a layer of spaghetti. Sprinkle remainder of cheese on top.
5. Cover and bake at 400° for about 20 minutes until bubbly.

SERVES 4.

Vegetables

Apricot Baked Beans

Nearly everyone loves baked beans. Adding apricots and bacon makes them an even more delicious treat.

OVEN   PREPARATION TIME: 1 HOUR

3 16-ounce cans pork and beans in tomato
  sauce, lightly drained
½ cup catsup
¼ cup instant minced onion
1 tablespoon horseradish
1 tablespoon prepared mustard

2 teaspoons Worcestershire sauce
1 17-ounce can apricot halves, drained
8 thick slices bacon (or 12 regular slices)
¼ cup packed light brown sugar
2 tablespoons melted butter

1. Stir together pork and beans, catsup, onions, horseradish, mustard, and Worcestershire in a
   shallow, 2½-quart ovenware casserole.
2. Alternately arrange drained apricot halves and bacon slices on top of bean mixture. Sprinkle
   with brown sugar.
3. Brushing apricots once or twice with butter, bake at 350° for 50 minutes or until bubbly.

SERVES 6.

Western Barbecue Beans

This delicious combination of vegetables and beans goes well with barbecued ribs, chicken, steak, or chops.

BARBECUE OR TOP BURNER   PREPARATION TIME: 20 MINUTES

2 tablespoons oil
1 large green pepper, chopped
½ pound mushrooms, thickly sliced
1 16-ounce can stewed tomatoes
1 20-ounce can kidney beans, drained

1 20-ounce can chick peas, drained
½ cup apricot preserves
2 tablespoons lemon juice
Salt

1. Heat oil in a skillet 6 inches above moderately hot coals (or on stove over moderate heat).
2. Sauté green pepper and mushrooms until tender but still crisp (about 5 minutes). Stir in all remaining ingredients except salt.
3. Stirring occasionally, bring mixture to a boil. Cook about 5 minutes more until piping hot. Season to taste with salt and serve.

SERVES 8.

Beets in Mustard Sauce

Here's a quick, tasty side dish for those hectic dinner hours.

NO COOKING   PREPARATION TIME: 10 MINUTES

1 1-pound can sliced beets
2 small red onions
1 tablespoon prepared mustard

1½ tablespoons white vinegar
½ cup sour cream
Pepper to taste

1. Drain the beets and place in a mixing bowl. Peel and slice onions and add them to the bowl.
2. Combine mustard, vinegar, sour cream, and pepper. Blend until smooth. Pour mixture over beets and toss well.

SERVES 4 TO 6.

Creamed Broccoli

For those special occasions, try this savory way of preparing a favorite side dish.

TOP BURNER   PREPARATION TIME: 25 MINUTES

1 bunch broccoli   2 tablespoons butter
Pinch baking soda   2 shallots, chopped
½ cup béchamel sauce   Salt and pepper
¼ cup heavy cream

1. Wash and clean broccoli and dry on paper towels. Boil enough water to cover broccoli, add baking soda. Add broccoli to boiling water and cook until tender. (Baking soda will keep broccoli green.)
2. Melt butter in small pan, add shallots, and sauté.
3. Cut cooked broccoli into small pieces and mix with béchamel sauce, heavy cream, and shallots. Salt and pepper to taste.

SERVES 4 TO 6

Polynesian Carrots

A zesty vegetable surprise that goes with anything from beef to chicken.

TOP BURNER   PREPARATION TIME: 20 MINUTES

1 tablespoon butter   1 tablespoon brown sugar
3 cups sliced carrots   1 teaspoon ginger
¾ cup water   1 tablespoon garlic salt
2 tablespoons white wine vinegar

1. Melt butter in a 10-inch frying pan. Add carrots, water, vinegar, sugar, ginger, and garlic salt.
2. Cover and simmer over moderately high heat for 12 to 15 minutes, or until carrots are just tender and liquid is absorbed.

SERVES 5 TO 6.

Creamed Cauliflower

This delicious French dish goes particularly well with lamb.

TOP BURNER   PREPARATION TIME: 20 MINUTES

1 head cauliflower
1 stick butter   Pinch nutmeg
1 tablespoon flour   ½ cup chicken stock
Salt to taste   Dash lemon juice
Pepper to taste   1 tablespoon heavy cream

1. Boil cauliflower in salted water until tender (about 5 to 7 minutes). Drain and mash with potato masher.
2. Melt butter in saucepan. Stir in flour and cook, stirring, for 5 minutes. Slowly add chicken stock, stirring constantly, until you have a sauce the consistency of heavy cream. Season to taste with salt, pepper, and nutmeg.
3. Add a drop or two of lemon juice and the heavy cream. Add cauliflower to the sauce and mix well. Turn onto serving plate and garnish with parsley.

SERVES 6.

Deviled Corn

Tabasco adds bite to this salty shore favorite.

BARBECUE   PREPARATION TIME: 20 MINUTES

6 ears corn   ½ cup chili sauce
½ cup butter   ½ teaspoon Tabasco

1. Fill a pail with sea water or heavily salted water. Pull back the shucks on corn and remove silk. Replace shucks and place corn into pail of water. Let soak for 30 minutes.
2. Drain corn and place on grill 8 inches above medium-hot coals. Grill until shucks are black. Turn and repeat until shucks are black all over.
3. Combine Tabasco and butter in small saucepan. Place 8 inches above medium coals, stirring until well blended. Serve over corn.

SERVES 6.

Grilled Eggplant Slices

Grilled eggplant is a new and delicious food for summer cookouts.

BARBECUE   PREPARATION TIME: 25 MINUTES

¼ cup melted butter
2 tablespoons grated Parmesan cheese
1 medium eggplant, unpeeled
Salt and pepper to taste

1. Melt butter in a saucepan. Remove from heat, and stir in grated Parmesan cheese. Slice unpeeled eggplant into slices about ⅜-inch thick.
2. Brush one side of all eggplant slices with butter and cheese mixture and lightly salt and pepper. Place on grill, buttered side down, about 6 inches above medium hot coals and cook 3 to 5 minutes until lightly browned.
3. Brush top side with butter mixture, turn with pancake turner, and grill about 5 minutes until browned and fork-tender. Remove and discard eggplant peel before eating.

SERVES 4.

Grilled Mushrooms

Once you try these grilled mushrooms, you'll never want to barbecue without them again.

BARBECUE   PREPARATION TIME: 15 MINUTES

18 large mushrooms
3 tablespoons melted butter

1. Carefully remove stems from mushrooms and save for use in stews, casseroles, etc. Brush mushroom caps with melted butter.
2. Place mushroom caps top side down on grill about 6 inches above medium hot coals. Brushing with butter twice, cook about 12 minutes or until tender. Do not turn. Serve with the juices which collect in mushrooms caps.

SERVES 4.

Melted Cheese Potatoes

This rich potato dish will go well with nearly any meat entree.

TOP BURNER

PREPARATION TIME: 35 MINUTES

2 pounds boiled, peeled potatoes
¼ cup butter
1 medium onion, sliced and separated into
   rings

2 tablespoons coarsely chopped pimiento
2 tablespoons coarsely chopped parsley
1 teaspoon salt
¾ cup grated Cheddar cheese

1. Melt butter in a medium skillet. Slice cooked potatoes into ⅛-inch slices.
2. Add potatoes, onion, pimiento, parsley, and salt to skillet and toss lightly to mix. Cover and cook over medium heat, stirring occasionally, until potatoes are heated and onions are tender-crisp—about 12 minutes.
3. Uncover skillet and sprinkle potatoes with ½ cup cheese. Cook uncovered an additional minute or two, stirring constantly, just until cheese is melted. Garnish with remaining ¼ cup cheese before serving.

SERVES 4.

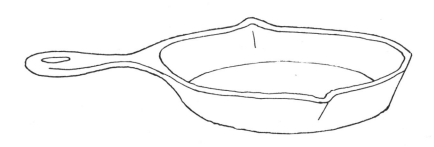

Potatoes Delmonico

OVEN   PREPARATION TIME: 30 MINUTES

3 tablespoons butter
3 tablespoons flour
¼ teaspoon salt
⅛ teaspoon white pepper
1½ cups milk

¾ cup onion salad dressing
5 medium potatoes, cooked, peeled,
   and diced
⅓ cup buttered bread crumbs

1. Preheat oven to 350°. Meanwhile, melt butter in medium saucepan and blend in flour, salt, and pepper. Gradually add milk and dressing, stirring constantly until mixture thickens. Combine with potatoes.
2. Pour into buttered 1½ quart baking dish. Top with buttered bread crumbs. Bake for 20 minutes at 350°.

SERVES 6.

Potatoes Florentine

A recipe for one of America's favorite dishes prepared with instant ingredients.

OVEN   PREPARATION TIME: 50 MINUTES

10- ounce package frozen spinach
2⅔ cups instant mashed potato flakes
2⅔ cups hot water
¼ cup butter or margarine

2 eggs
¼ cup grated Parmesan cheese
1 teaspoon salt
Pepper to taste

1. Thaw spinach enough to separate leaves and drain.
2. Mix potato flakes and water in a large bowl and let stand until flakes soak up water.
3. Add butter, eggs, cheese, salt, and pepper to potatoes and mix well. Fold in the spinach. Pour mixture into a greased baking pan or dish.
4. Bake at 350° for 40 minutes.

SERVES 6.

Sweet Potatoes Baked In Brandy

Sweet and flavorful, with unexpected contrasts of taste and texture.

OVEN   PREPARATION TIME: 40 MINUTES

2 2-pound cans sweet potatoes
1 1-pound can pineapple chunks
½ cup walnut halves
2 tablespoons butter
1 cup packed brown sugar

¼ cup brandy
½ teaspoon cinnamon
¼ teaspoon nutmeg
¼ teaspoon salt

1. Drain sweet potatoes and spread out in a flat 2-quart casserole.
2. Drain pineapple. Arrange chunks over sweet potatoes. Sprinkle walnut halves over all.
3. Melt butter. Blend in brown sugar, brandy, cinnamon, nutmeg, and salt. Pour over sweet potatoes. Bake uncovered in a 375° oven for 30 minutes.

SERVES 6 TO 8.

Broiled Tomatoes

Here's an easy way to add a colorful, hot vegetable dish to any meal.

BROILER   PREPARATION TIME: 10 MINUTES

3 large ripe tomatoes
Salt and pepper to taste
2 teaspoons butter
2 teaspoons fine dry breadcrumbs

1. Wash tomatoes, cut off stem ends, and cut tomatoes into 1-inch slices.
2. Place slices on broiler rack or in broiler pan. Sprinkle with salt and pepper, dot each slice with butter, and sprinkle with breadcrumbs.
3. Broil 5 to 7 minutes until tomatoes are soft and crumbs slightly browned.

SERVES 6.

Grilled Tomatoes

While barbecuing steak or hamburgers, cook these tomatoes, deliciously accented with dill, at the side of the grill.

BARBECUE   PREPARATION TIME: 15 MINUTES

2 tablespoons butter
½ teaspoon dried dill weed
2 large tomatoes

1. Melt the butter and stir in the dill weed. Cut the two large tomatoes in half and brush the cut sides with the butter sauce.
2. Place tomatoes, cut sides down, on grill about 6 inches above medium hot coals and cook about 5 minutes until lightly browned.
3. Brush skin sides of tomatoes with butter sauce and turn with pancake turner. Brush cut sides with butter sauce. Grill 7 minutes longer until tomatoes are fork tender and serve immediately.

SERVES 4.

Turnips Au Gratin

OVEN   PREPARATION TIME: 35 MINUTES

2 tablespoons butter   1 cup milk
2 tablespoons flour   3 cups diced cooked turnips
¼ teaspoon salt   1 cup (4 ounces) shredded Cheddar cheese

1. Melt butter in a saucepan. Stir in flour and salt until smooth. Add milk slowly, stirring rapidly. Continuing to stir, bring mixture to a boil.
2. Gently mix white sauce and turnips and pour into a baking dish. Sprinkle with cheese and bake in 375° oven about 20 minutes, or until cheese melts.

SERVES 6.

Timetable for Cooking Vegetables

VEGETABLE	COOKING TIME
Corn (frozen), Tomatoes (sliced)	4 to 5 minutes
Corn-on-the-cob	5 to 6 minutes
Carrots (canned), Zucchini (sliced)	5 to 7 minutes
Beets (sliced), Broccoli (fresh), Cabbage (chopped), Carrots (sliced), Onions (small, whole), Peas (fresh or canned), Sauerkraut	6 to 8 minutes
Green peppers (sliced)	6 to 9 minutes
Spinach (canned)	7 to 8 minutes
Asparagus (canned), Beans (green, fresh)	7 to 10 minutes
Beans (green, canned), Brussels sprouts (canned), Carrots (frozen), Celery (fresh), Spinach (fresh or frozen)	8 to 10 minutes
Asparagus (whole, fresh or frozen)	8 to 12 minutes
Beans (green, frozen), Brussels sprouts (frozen), Peas (frozen)	10 to 12 minutes
Cabbage (small, quartered)	10 to 15 minutes
Brussels sprouts (fresh)	12 to 14 minutes
Cauliflower (quartered)	12 to 15 minutes
Mushrooms (whole, fresh)	14 to 16 minutes
Potatoes (small, whole)	14 to 18 minutes
Artichokes (whole)	18 to 20 minutes

Sauces

Béchamel Sauce

Wonderful things happen when you mix this basic sauce with drippings from beef or chicken.

TOP BURNER

PREPARATION TIME: 15 MINUTES

2 tablespoons butter
2 tablespoons flour
1 cup chicken broth

¼ cup red wine
Salt and pepper to taste

1. Melt butter in a saucepan. Add flour and cook over low heat until flour turns brown.
2. Add chicken broth and wine slowly. Bring to a boil, and season with salt and pepper to taste.

MAKES 1 CUP.

Buttery Herb Sauce

Add this sauce to hot cooked spaghetti or egg noodles and toss lightly until thoroughly mixed. Serve the spaghetti as a main course or as a side dish.

NO COOKING   PREPARATION TIME: 15 MINUTES

½ cup softened butter   2 teaspoons chopped chives
½ cup grated Parmesan cheese   1½ teaspoons grated lemon rind
1 tablespoon chopped parsley   1 teaspoon paprika
1 tablespoon lemon juice

1. Combine all ingredients in a small bowl. Mix thoroughly.
2. Add sauce to hot linguine, spaghetti, or egg noodles and toss lightly.

MAKES 1 CUP.

Cheese and Nut Sauce

The delicate flavor of this unusual sauce enhances nearly any pasta dish.

NO COOKING   PREPARATION TIME: 15 MINUTES

1 cup firmly packed chopped parsley   2 tablespoons boiling water
¾ cup grated Parmesan cheese   1 tablespoon basil leaves
½ cup olive oil   1 teaspoon salt
¼ cup finely chopped walnuts   ⅛ teaspoon pepper
2 tablespoons butter   2 cloves garlic, mashed

1. Combine all ingredients and mix thoroughly in a small bowl. (Or combine all ingredients in a blender and blend at medium speed until well mixed.)
2. Add sauce to hot cooked macaroni, spaghetti, linguine, or egg noodles and toss lightly until thoroughly mixed.

MAKES ABOUT 1½ CUPS.

Delicious Fruit Sauce

This sauce, which can be used hot or cold, makes an excellent topping for pancakes, ice cream, cake, custard, or pudding.

TOP BURNER   PREPARATION TIME: 15 MINUTES

2 to 4 tablespoons sugar (to taste)   1 tablespoon lemon juice
2 tablespoons cornstarch   1 cup drained and crushed canned fruit
2 cups liquid from canned fruits   (optional)

1. Mix sugar and cornstarch in a small pan and stir in fruit liquid.
2. Stirring constantly, cook over low heat until thickened. Stir in lemon juice and crushed fruit (if used).

MAKES 2 CUPS (3 CUPS WITH FRUIT).

Remoulade

Spread it on cold meats and shellfish; mix it into vegetables and salads—in its thousand and one uses, this sauce is a winner every time.

NO COOKING   PREPARATION TIME: 20 MINUTES

1 tablespoon powdered mustard   1 teaspoon onion powder
1 teaspoon warm water   1 teaspoon capers
1 cup mayonnaise   1 teaspoon parsley flakes
1 tablespoon sweet pickle relish   ¼ teaspoon crumbled tarragon leaves

1. In a small cup, combine mustard with water. Let stand 10 minutes for flavor to develop.
2. Blend mustard with remaining ingredients. Mix well.

MAKES ABOUT 1 CUP.

Seafood Curry Sauce

Spicy and piquant, this sauce will make noodles stand up and holler "Howdy!"

TOP BURNER   PREPARATION TIME: 20 MINUTES

¼ cup chopped onion
4 tablespoons butter
4 tablespoons flour
1 to 2 tablespoons curry powder
½ teaspoon salt
Dash pepper

Dash paprika
2½ cups milk
2 tablespoons lemon juice
1 to 2 cups cooked shrimp, crab, or lobster
1 package noodles

1. Sauté onion in butter until light brown.
2. Blend in flour and seasonings. Add milk. Cook, stirring constantly, until sauce thickens.
3. Add lemon juice and shellfish; heat through. Serve over cooked noodles.

MAKES 4 TO 5 CUPS.

Spicy Barbecue Sauce

Keep this basting sauce handy whenever you're barbecuing chicken, beef, lamb, veal, or pork.

TOP BURNER   PREPARATION TIME: 10 MINUTES

1 cup tomato juice
¼ cup wine vinegar
2 tablespoons brown sugar
1 tablespoon cornstarch
1 tablespoon instant minced onion
1 tablespoon salad oil

1 teaspoon powdered mustard
1 teaspoon salt
½ teaspoon garlic powder
¼ teaspoon ground red pepper
1 chicken or beef bouillon cube

1. Combine all ingredients in a small saucepan and bring to a boil.
2. Stirring constantly, cook for about 3 minutes until mixture thickens.

MAKES 1½ CUPS.

Tangy Tartar Sauce

Prepare this sauce in advance for your next fish dinner.

NO COOKING   PREPARATION TIME: 5 MINUTES

½ cup mayonnaise or salad dressing   1 tablespoon chopped parsley
1 tablespoon chopped olives   1 tablespoon chopped sweet pickle
1 tablespoon chopped onion

1. Combine all ingredients and mix well.
2. Chill and serve with fish.

MAKES ABOUT ¾ CUP.

Teriyaki Sauce

A quick way to prepare a snappy sauce which can be used for marinating steak or chicken.

NO COOKING   PREPARATION TIME: 10 MINUTES

½ cup soy sauce   ½ teaspoon ground ginger
¼ cup white wine   ¼ teaspoon garlic powder
2 tablespoons sugar

1. Blend together all ingredients and stir until sugar dissolves.
2. Brush sauce on steak or chicken during grilling.

MAKES ¾ CUP.

Desserts

Baked Apples

Here's an easy way to have sugary baked apples ready for dessert when you're barbecuing outdoors.

BARBECUE   PREPARATION TIME: 1 HOUR

4 medium cooking apples, cored   ½ cup raisins
½ cup brown sugar   Water
2 teaspoons butter   Heavy cream (optional)

1. Cut about 1 inch of peel from the top of each apple. Stand each apple on a piece of heavy duty foil (or double layer of regular foil) large enough to cover apple completely.
2. Fill the core of each apple with 1 to 2 tablespoons brown sugar, ½ teaspoon butter, and a few raisins.
3. Bring corners of foil together over apple and spoon 1½ teaspoons water into each foil packet. Seal edges of foil with apples standing right side up.
4. Place foil-wrapped apples right side up around edge of coals and bake for 45 to 55 minutes. Rotate apples 2 or 3 times during baking period so all sides bake evenly, taking care that apples remain right side up.
5. Apples are done when they pierce easily with a fork. To serve, remove from foil and place in bowl with remaining syrup from foil packet. Cover with heavy cream, if desired.

SERVES 4.

Berries In Wine

This crisp mixture of fruit tastes can't be beat for a summer dessert.

TOP BURNER

PREPARATION TIME: 25 MINUTES

½ cup sugar
½ cup water
½ cup red Beaujolais, Burgundy, or
   Bordeaux wine

1 pint fresh strawberries
1 pint fresh blueberries
1 pint raspberries

1. Wash and clean strawberries, blueberries, and raspberries, and put them aside in separate containers.
2. Mix sugar, water, and wine in a saucepan and simmer for 5 minutes.
3. Mix strawberries and blueberries in a glass bowl and top with raspberries.
4. Pour the wine syrup over the berries. Chill in refrigerator for 3 to 4 hours before serving.

SERVES 6.

Blueberry Pancakes

A breakfast dish for dessert? Try it!

TOP BURNER

PREPARATION TIME: 30 MINUTES

1½ cups fresh blueberries
2 cups flour
2 tablespoons sugar
4 teaspoons double-acting baking powder

½ teaspoon salt
2 lightly beaten eggs
1¾ cups milk
6 tablespoons melted butter

1. Wash and clean blueberries in cold water and gently pat dry on paper towels.
2. Prepare batter by combining flour, sugar, baking powder, and salt in a deep mixing bowl. Mix in the eggs, milk, and 2 tablespoons of the cooled, melted butter. Batter does not have to be too smooth. Gently stir blueberries into batter mixture.
3. Grease a large, heavy griddle or skillet with the remaining butter and warm over moderate heat. Fry 3 or 4 pancakes at a time, turning once, until golden brown on each side.

SERVES 4.

Brandy Alexander Pie

To bring those special evenings to a memorable end, you can't do better than this elegant dessert.

TOP BURNER

PREPARATION TIME: 35 MINUTES

1 envelope unflavored gelatin
½ cup cold water
⅔ cup sugar
⅛ teaspoon salt
3 eggs, separated

¼ cup cognac
¼ cup crème de cacao
2 cups heavy cream
1 9-inch graham cracker pie crust

1. Sprinkle the gelatin over the cold water in a saucepan, and blend in ⅓ cup of sugar, the salt, and egg yolks. Heat over low heat, stirring constantly, until gelatin is dissolved, but do not boil.
2. Remove from heat. Stir in the cognac and crème de cacao. Chill until mixture becomes very thick.
3. Beat egg whites until stiff, adding the remaining sugar. Fold the egg whites into the chilled yolk mixture.
4. Whip 1 cup of heavy cream and fold into mixture. Pour the mixture into the pie crust.
5. Chill for several hours and garnish with the remaining cream.

SERVES 6 TO 8.

Brandy Alexander Soufflé

The alcohol cooks away, leaving the delectable essence of mingled brandy and chocolate.

TOP BURNER   PREPARATION TIME: 40 MINUTES

2 envelopes unflavored gelatin   1 8-ounce package cream cheese
1¾ cups cold water   3 tablespoons brandy
1 cup sugar   3 tablespoons crème de cacao
4 eggs, separated   1 cup heavy cream, whipped

1. Soften gelatin in 1 cup water. Stir over low heat until dissolved.
2. Add remaining water. Remove from heat. Blend in ¾ cup sugar and beaten egg yolks. Return to heat. Cook 2 to 3 minutes.
3. Gradually add mixture to softened cream cheese, mixing until well blended. Stir in brandy and crème de cacao. Stir until slightly thickened. Beat egg whites until foamy. Gradually add remaining sugar, beating until stiff peaks form.
4. Fold egg whites and whipped cream into cream cheese mixture. Pour mixture into 1½-quart soufflé dish. Chill until firm. Garnish with nutmeg or chocolate shavings, if desired.

SERVES 8 TO 10.

Chocolate Chiffon

For chocolate lovers on a diet—here's one dessert that doesn't taste like diet food.

TOP BURNER

PREPARATION TIME: 30 MINUTES

1 envelope unflavored gelatin
½ cup cold water
⅔ cup nonfat dry milk
1¼ cups cold water

2 teaspoons chocolate extract
½ teaspoon vanilla extract
½ teaspoon liquid artificial sweetener

1. Combine gelatin with ½ cup cold water.
2. Stir dry milk into 1¼ cups cold water. Heat to boiling. Remove from heat.
3. Add gelatin and stir to dissolve. Stir in extracts and artificial sweetener. Chill until partially set.
4. Using electric mixer or rotary beater, whip until foamy. Spoon into sherbet glasses.

MAKES 7 CUPS.

Chocolate Mousse

A perfect recipe for this fluffy, chocolaty, classic French dessert.

TOP BURNER

PREPARATION TIME: 40 MINUTES

4 eggs, separated
¾ cup sugar
¼ cup Grand Marnier
6 ounces semi-sweet chocolate bits

4 tablespoons instant coffee
1 stick soft butter
1 cup heavy cream
1 tablespoon sugar

1. In a double boiler, add ¾ cup sugar to egg yolks and cook over low heat until sugar is melted. Add the Grand Marnier and set aside.
2. In a small saucepan, melt the chocolate with the instant coffee. Over a low heat add the butter bit by bit to the chocolate mixture.
3. Add the chocolate mixture to the egg yolks.
4. Beat egg whites until stiff, adding 1 tablespoon sugar, and fold into egg yolk mixture. Refrigerate until well chilled.

SERVES 4 TO 6.

Chocolate Oatmeal Cookies

Everybody's favorite—they'll be gone before you know it.

OVEN

PREPARATION TIME: 45 MINUTES

2 cups sugar
½ cup unsweetened cocoa
½ cup butter
½ cup milk
½ teaspoon salt
3 cups quick-cooking oatmeal

1 cup chopped walnuts
1 teaspoon ground cinnamon
½ teaspoon ground nutmeg
2 teaspoons pure vanilla extract
2 beaten eggs

1. In a saucepan large enough for mixing cookies, combine sugar, cocoa, butter, milk, and salt. Mix well.
2. Stir and cook over medium heat for 3 to 4 minutes. Remove from heat and stir in oatmeal, walnuts, cinnamon, nutmeg, and vanilla extract. Mix well.
3. Blend in eggs. Drop by teaspoonful onto lightly greased cookie sheet. Bake in a 350° oven for 10 minutes. Remove immediately from cookie sheets to cooling racks.

MAKES ABOUT 6 DOZEN COOKIES.

Cinnamon Apple Rings

These sweet, pan-fried apple rings make a deliciously different accompaniment to most meats.

TOP BURNER

PREPARATION TIME: 20 MINUTES

3 large cooking apples
3 tablespoons butter

1 tablespoon sugar
½ teaspoon cinnamon

1. Wash and core the apples. Slice apples into ½-inch thick rings.
2. Melt butter in frying pan. Place apples in melted butter and fry slowly over moderately low heat until tender (about 10 to 12 minutes), turning once to brown evenly.
3. Sprinkle apples with mixture of sugar and cinnamon before serving.

SERVES 6.

French Strawberry Cake

Strawberries and cream—an American favorite turned into a classic of Gallic cuisine.

NO COOKING   PREPARATION TIME: 40 MINUTES

1 pint fresh strawberries
2 tablespoons sugar
3 teaspoons pure vanilla extract
1 10-inch angel food cake

1 3¾-ounce package instant vanilla pudding
  mix
1¾ cups milk
1 cup heavy cream, whipped

1. Wash, hull, and slice strawberries. Sprinkle with sugar and 1 teaspoon of the vanilla. Let stand 30 minutes.
2. Cut a ½-inch-thick layer from the top of the cake and set aside. From bottom portion remove the center, leaving a ½-inch shell around sides and bottom. Crumble pieces removed from center to make 1½ cups crumbs; set aside.
3. In a small mixing bowl, combine pudding mix, milk, and the remaining 2 teaspoons vanilla. Beat until smooth (mixture will be thin). Let stand about 5 minutes to thicken. Fold in strawberries, cake crumbs, and half of the whipped cream.
4. Spoon mixture into shell. Replace top layer. Garnish with remaining whipped cream. Chill.

SERVES 12.

Fruit Pudding

PREPARATION TIME: 20 MINUTES

1 egg
¼ cup sugar
3 tablespoons cornstarch
½ teaspoon salt
2 cups milk

1 tablespoon butter
1 teaspoon vanilla
2 cups canned fruit cocktail or drained canned peaches
½ teaspoon cinnamon

1. Beat egg in saucepan and stir in sugar, cornstarch, and salt.
2. Stir in milk. Stirring constantly, cook over medium heat until thickened. Cook and stir one minute longer.
3. Stir in butter and vanilla. Add fruit to pudding.
4. Cool and sprinkle with cinnamon before serving.

SERVES 6.

Grilled Pecan Sundae

Barbecued ice cream? This recipe will make you a convert—and add an unexpected touch to your cookouts.

BARBECUE

PREPARATION TIME: 10 MINUTES

¼ cup butter
1 cup firmly packed dark brown sugar
1 cup blended maple syrup

1 6-ounce can pecan halves
2 pints vanilla ice cream

1. In saucepan, combine all ingredients except for ice cream. Place on grill over medium-hot coals.
2. Stirring constantly, heat until sauce bubbles. Let simmer gently for 5 minutes.
3. Scoop vanilla ice cream into serving dishes. Spoon hot sauce over ice cream. Serve at once.

SERVES 6.

Mocha Chiffon Pie

You'll think you're in sunny Jamaica when you bite into this mouth-watering concoction of coffee and chocolate.

TOP BURNER

PREPARATION TIME: 40 MINUTES

1 envelope unflavored gelatin
¼ cup cold water
1 cup milk
3 eggs, separated
½ cup sugar
2 tablespoons cocoa

1 tablespoon instant coffee
⅛ teaspoon mace
Few grains salt
¼ cup sugar
¼ teaspoon cream of tartar
1 9-inch graham cracker crust

1. Soften gelatin in cold water. Scald milk in top of double boiler.
2. Beat egg yolks slightly; mix in the ½ cup sugar, cocoa, coffee, mace, and salt. Stir a little hot milk into egg yolk mixture.
3. Pour egg yolk-milk mixture into remaining hot milk. Cook over hot water, stirring, until it thickens. Remove from heat, add gelatin, and stir until completely dissolved. Cool.
4. Beat egg whites until foamy; add cream of tartar and continue to beat until fairly stiff. Gradually beat in the ¼ cup sugar, continuing to beat until soft peaks form. Fold into cooled mixture.
5. Pour into pie crust. Chill until firm. Garnish with whipped cream.

SERVES 6 TO 8.

Peaches in Champagne

This elegant offering provides both a drink and a perky dessert.

NO COOKING   PREPARATION TIME: 10 MINUTES

6 fresh ripe peaches
1 bottle dry champagne

1. Peel the peaches and place each one in a large goblet. Prick the flesh of the peach all over with a fork and cover with champagne.
2. Drink the champagne and eat the peach for dessert.

SERVES 6.

Perfect Peach Pie

You can't go wrong with this one—comes out right every time.

TOP BURNER   PREPARATION TIME: 45 MINUTES

1 baked 9-inch pastry shell
1 can sliced peaches, chilled
2 3-inch pieces cinnamon
1 envelope unflavored gelatin

3 egg whites
¼ teaspoon cream of tartar
¼ cup sugar

1. Drain peach slices, saving the juice. Cut all but six into small pieces and put aside.
2. Put ½ cup of the juice and cinnamon in top of double boiler and heat 30 minutes. Remove cinnamon.
3. Soften gelatin in ¼ cup of the juice. Add to heated juice, stirring until gelatin dissolves. Cool.
4. While mixture is cooling, combine egg whites and cream of tartar in mixing bowl. Beat until foamy.
5. Add sugar gradually, beating the mixture until stiff peaks form. Gently fold egg whites into gelatin mixture. Chill 5 minutes. Fold in peaches. Fill pie shell. Chill until set. Decorate top with peach slices.

SERVES 6 TO 8.

Strawberries and Wine

This refreshing summery dessert is simplicity itself to prepare.

2 pints fresh strawberries
Sugar to taste
1 cup rosé wine

1. Wash and hull strawberries. Place them in a glass bowl and sugar to taste.
2. Pour the wine onto the strawberries and mix lightly. Let stand several hours before serving.

SERVES 4.

Strawberry Malt

Extra rich and creamy—a quick pick-me-up at the end of a long day's ride.

NO COOKING   PREPARATION TIME: 5 MINUTES

1 pint fresh strawberries
1 pint softened vanilla ice cream
2 tablespoons instant malted milk powder
1 tablespoon pure vanilla extract

1. Puree strawberries in blender. Add ice cream, malted milk powder, and vanilla extract. Blend until smooth.
2. Serve in tall glasses with long spoons. Garnish with fresh strawberries, if desired.

SERVES 3.

Strawberry Topping Supreme

Spoon it over cake, ice cream, or fresh sliced peaches—this versatile topping will be everyone's favorite.

NO COOKING   PREPARATION TIME: 10 MINUTES PLUS CHILLING TIME

1 pint fresh strawberries, halved
¼ cup sherry
¼ teaspoon cinnamon

⅛ teaspoon nutmeg
6 slices pound cake
Whipped cream

1. Mix together strawberries, sherry, cinnamon, and nutmeg. Chill.
2. Spoon mixture over cake slices. Top with whipped cream.

SERVES 6.

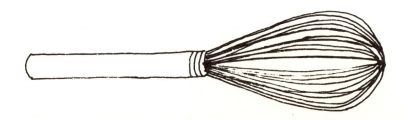

Sunshine Lemon Pie

Tart and creamy—a pie your whole family will enjoy.

TOP BURNER

PREPARATION TIME: 40 MINUTES

1 package unflavored gelatin
¼ cup cold water
4 eggs, separated
1 cup sugar
½ cup lemon juice

½ teaspoon salt
½ teaspoon grated lemon peel
½ teaspoon ground nutmeg
⅓ cup whipped heavy cream
1 9-inch baked pie shell

1. In a cup, soften gelatin in water. Set aside.
2. In the top of a double boiler, beat egg yolks until thick and lemon-colored. Gradually beat in ½ cup of the sugar, lemon juice, and salt. Cook, stirring continuously, over hot water until custard coats a metal spoon (about 10 minutes).
3. Remove from heat and stir in softened gelatin, mixing until gelatin is dissolved. Blend in lemon peel and nutmeg. Chill until slightly thickened.
4. Beat egg whites until they stand in soft peaks. Gradually beat in remaining ½ cup sugar. Beat until stiff but not dry.
5. Fold into gelatin mixture. Fold in whipped cream. Turn into pie shell. Chill until firm and ready to serve. Garnish with whipped cream and lemon slices.

MAKES 6 TO 8 SERVINGS.

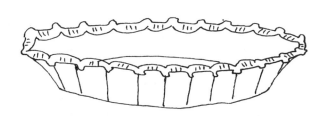

Sweet Wine Melon

Wine and melon make a perfect match for delicious summertime desserts.

NO COOKING   PREPARATION TIME: 10 MINUTES

1 ripe honeydew melon
½ cup Sauternes or Barsac wine

1. Cut a plug from the stem end of the melon and scoop out the seeds.
2. Pour the wine into the melon through the hole, and replace the plug. Refrigerate for 1 hour.
3. To serve, spoon the melon and mingled juices into individual bowls.

SERVES 4.